Susan North

Also by Dr. Georgia Witkin:

Human Sexuality
The Female Stress Syndrome
The Male Stress Syndrome

Quick Fixes & Small Comforts

QUICK FIXES

&

SMALL COMFORTS

HOW EVERY WOMAN CAN RESIST THOSE IRRESISTIBLE URGES

Georgia Witkin, Ph.D.

Villard Books   New York   1988

Library of Congress Cataloging-in-Publication Data

Witkin, Georgia.
Quick fixes and small comforts.
1. Compulsive behavior.   2. Dependency
(Psychology)   3. Women—United States—
Substance use.   4. Women—United States—
Psychology.   I. Title.
RC451.4.w6w57   1988   616.85′227′088042   87-40572
ISBN 0-394-56040-x

In order to protect patient confidentiality, cases are
composites and do not reflect any one individual.

Designed by Marysarah Quinn

Manufactured in the United States of America
9 8 7 6 5 4 3 2
FIRST EDITION

TO THE WOMEN IN MY LIFE
WHO OFFER REAL FIXES AND GREAT COMFORT:

Anne Johnson
Diane Reverend
Esther Newberg
Joan Lippert Indig
Connie Freeman
Bobby Gallagher
Patricia Schreiner-Engel
Blanche Ross
Dee Ann Mernet
Grada Fischer
Gail Steinberg
Patricia Paddison
Barbara Lane
Birgitte Mednick
Natalie Weinstein

AND TO THE WONDERFUL WOMEN IN MY FAMILY:

Mildred Witkin-Radovic
Anne Witkin
Linda Perlman
Laurie Witkin
Nikki Witkin
Jenny Witkin

And to My Daughter Kimberly, with All My Love

Appreciation

AT&T Corporation, New York, New York

Abbott Northwestern Hospital, Minneapolis, Minnesota

Baptist Medical Center, Columbia, South Carolina

Booz, Allen and Hamilton, New York, New York

Charter Glade Hospital, Fort Myers, Florida

Charter Hills Hospital, Greensboro, North Carolina

Edward Hospital Woman's Center for Health, Naperville, Illinois

Health Connection, Des Moines, Iowa

Health Magazine, New York, New York

Mercy Health and Education Corporation, Albany, New York

Mercy Hospital Women's Health Connection, Des Moines, Iowa

Mount Sinai Medical College, New York, New York

Nashville Women's Health Center, Nashville, Tennessee

Rose Medical Center, Denver, Colorado

Appreciation

Sarasota Mental Health Association, Sarasota, Florida

Timken Mercy Medical Center, Canton, Ohio

United Jersey Bank Women's Bureau, Saddle Brook, New Jersey

Western Baptist Hospital Women's Center, Paducah, Kentucky

Wilson College, Chambersburg, Pennsylvania

Contents

Introduction

Is a dish of chocolate ice cream with fudge sauce on top irresistible to you after a frustrating day?

Do you get a glow of glamour from buying a pair of satin dress shoes on sale even though you haven't been to a formal in three years?

Does a new lipstick make you forget that you are overdrawn on your checking account—for a few minutes?

Is a telephone call each hour the only way you can get through the day?

Are you repainting your outdoor furniture at two in the morning for no earthly reason known to you?

Did you go house hunting with your husband the week after you finally decided to divorce him?

Is a sleeping pill something you really don't need but take each night just in case you might be sleepless?

Does your living room get rearranged every time you end a romance?

Explaining women's buying binges, cookie sprees, and cleaning marathons as masochistic asks us to believe that we enjoy suffering. Interpreting our compulsive behaviors as an indication that we are out of control by temperament tells us that we will always be feeling guilt-ridden and self-punishing.

An endless number of popular books on best-seller lists are saying just that. They say that we are most likely to love those men who love us the least. That our generally good judgment in human relations disappears when we are making life choices. That our eating, shopping, smoking, drinking, yelling, and telephoning impulses mean that we can't deal with the stresses of a "man's world" and that we are about to self-destruct.

I see these behaviors as quick fixes and small comforts. I think these behaviors are attempts to make things better, not worse. I think that women who give at the office and give at home need to *take* in order to keep going. We have not been raised to make our problems priorities. We have been raised to try to be perfect. And perfect people don't have problems. So we try to solve our problems quickly, quietly, and by ourselves.

We parent our parents, our spouses, and our children. We buy their clothes, prepare their food, listen to their problems, and give them love. Is it any wonder that women buy themselves clothes, feed themselves food, talk on the telephone, and want some tender loving care themselves? Women are not exhibiting "dependencies" when we reach for fast remedies like chocolate, charge cards, or chats. We are exhibiting "independencies." We are trying to fill our own needs, take care of ourselves—and fast. Fast so that we can keep going, fast so that the time spent on ourselves will not interfere with the time we spend on others, and fast so that no one will know that we, too, are needy. We reach for quick fixes and small comforts.

Quick fixes and small comforts, though, do not fix our problems at all. The sugar high that fixes our fatigue for the moment can lead us to post-candy lows within the hour. Home-style pasta that makes us feel "home again" for the evening makes us feel fat in the morning. The small presents we buy ourselves all month add up to debt and guilt at the end of the month. The extra cup of coffee, cigarette, drink, or tranquilizer that does seem to help in the short run only hurts us in the long run. These instant remedies harm not only our bodies but our sense of control as well. We then face the original problems we tried to fix quickly, and the problems the fixes gave us.

The problem with quick fixes is that these small comforts may develop into compelling compulsions. A compulsion is a recurrent, persistent impulse, difficult or impossible to resist. Eating, for example, may be just an activity that satisfies hunger at mealtimes. Then eating is non-compulsive. What we eat and how much we eat is a choice. Eating, however, may also be a tension reliever, and snacking is a compulsion difficult to resist. Finally, eating may be a constant preoccupation, and gorging is then a compulsion impossible to control. If eating is fixing your hunger, no problem. If eating is a substitute for comfort you really need from praise or attention, a problem is beginning. If eating seems to be the only fix to all your tensions, a definite problem exists.

If the quick fix or small comfort we reach for to help us keep going becomes a compulsion, we lose our sense of control over our own behavior. Since we reached for the fix because we already felt some part of our life was broken or out of control, we now feel even more overwhelmed. In my survey of 1,661 women across the country, each reported at least one fix which had become a problem for them to control. Who were these women? They live in California, Iowa, Kentucky, Illinois, New Jersey, Tennessee, New York, Florida, Connecticut, Minnesota, Colorado, Massachusetts, Ohio, North Carolina, Washington, D.C., and South Carolina. They work inside and outside their homes. About one in five is a full-time homemaker or retiree who is now home full time. The others list their occupations as follows:

FULL-TIME OCCUPATIONS

*Office supervisor
*Office manager
*Registered nurse
*Secretary
*Data processor
*Student (college, master's,
  doctoral)
Insurance broker
Teacher
Dietician
Professor
Engineer
Banking officer
Purchasing agent
Dentist
Bookkeeper

Psychologist
Personal benefits
Advertising (coordinator,
  producer)
Administrative assistant
Nursing supervisor
Receptionist
Retail manager
Police department clerk
Factory assembly-line worker
Hotel catering manager
Office clerk/accountant
Hospital vice president
Physician

* *Most frequently listed.*

PART-TIME OCCUPATIONS

*Substitute teacher
*Student (college, master's,
  doctoral)
*Registered nurse
*Counselor
Librarian
Speech pathologist
Pediatrician
Author
Photographer

Musician
Proofreader
Exotic dancer
Auctioneer
Massage therapist
Fitness instructor
Actress
Law student
Audiologist
Mail carrier

* *Most frequently mentioned.*

Is this a random sample? That is, did every woman in the United States have an equal chance of being picked for this survey? No. It is a self-selected sample of women. That is, women in the survey *chose* to attend my Women's Health Day keynote address or seminar in their city and also *chose* to fill out and hand in the survey form on Quick Fixes and Small Comforts. Many, therefore, were particularly stressed, or interested in stress management and women's wellness. If you are too, they are probably very much like you. But it is also a *representative* sample of women across the country, across age groups, across marital and non-marital statuses, and across occupations. Since, indeed, the sample is representative, much of what you read will be familiar and helpful. If you are one of the women who participated in the survey or granted me an in-depth interview, thank you! If you are new to this study, read on.

The fixes and comforts these women most often mentioned included shopping, eating, telephoning, yelling, napping, smoking, drinking, gambling, fantasizing, cleaning, having affairs, using drugs, watching television, working too hard, and constantly redecorating. Do they sound familiar?

Some are so embarrassing to us that we make them "secret fixes"—night eating, for example, or masturbating.

Some are "big fixes" because they are quick to plan but turn out to be very slow in execution. A new house to revitalize a relationship. A new baby to bond a marriage. Other fixes come with potions, lotions, and the magic mirror images of our childhood fairy tales. The diet-do-over is one example. The makeup makeover is another. Change our hair and we will be changed, they tell us. A quick fix, I call it.

Fixes that can kill are, of course, the most frightening of all. Even when they don't kill, they always add new problems to old. When we drink to forget, for example, we instead make time stand still. We do not move on. So we try more alcohol. Is this self-destructive behavior? Not in its motivation. We are moved to make ourselves feel better, forget, or forgive. We are left, however, having taken steps backward.

Sedatives, tranquilizers, stimulants, and hallucinogenics are less socially sanctioned than alcohol but also likely to be abused. If we are down on energy or optimism, we may try to raise our spirits to normal with coffee, cigarettes, amphetamines, or cocaine. If we are too high on tension, we try to bring ourselves down into functioning range with painkillers, sleeping pills, muscle relaxants, or mood mellowers.

Again and again, we do patch jobs on our feelings, our bodies, and our lives. We try for quick fixes and small comforts instead of real remedies since the one person in the world we have too little time for is *ourselves*. And the patches peel off. So we patch and patch again. We are action-oriented and we are earnest, but with best intentions we are making our lives worse. With each impulsive-compulsive attempt to regain our sense of control, we lose more real control. Each hour shopping spree leads to months of balancing bills. Each secret candy bar, chocolate cake, and slice of pizza leads to hours of guilt and weeks of weight watching. Each drink and pill to make us feel better now adds up to trouble later. It is time to stop the quick fixes and do it right.

- Recognize that a need for a "fix" means something needs fixing! In the chapters to come you will learn what types of problems are most often associated with particular fixes.
- Recognize that compulsive, out-of-control behaviors are always *symptoms* of a syndrome. Let's not pretend that the fixes are our only concern. "If I could just stay away from singles bars, my life would be different," I hear. Or, "If I didn't take so many tranquilizers . . ." We will talk about *why* you may be craving sex or sedatives. Only then can you really change behaviors that bring momentary sweet nothings into behaviors that bring self-esteem.

- Recognize that makeovers don't last and do-overs don't exist. After you learn about your fixes and their sources, you will still be you. And that's okay! With humor and patience, we can all learn to manage our impulses. Perhaps even indulge ourselves from time to time by choice!

Quick Fixes & Small Comforts

ONE

What Is a Fix?

What is a "fix"? We use the term lightly to refer to our morning cup of coffee. We use the term with concern when we talk about drug addiction, and with disdain when we talk about gossiping. We all have our "fixes," and refer to ourselves affectionately as stimulus junkies, telephone junkies, bargain addicts, or junk-food junkies. Not many of us have given much thought to what such fixes really are.

Fixes are *behaviors*, behaviors that we:

- rely upon to keep ourselves going at a fast pace;
- indulge in to make ourselves feel better rather than face feeling bad;
- employ to block upsetting thoughts or feelings so that we can continue to look as cheerful as we think we are expected to look;
- use to displace anger or frustration from those we think we should love to those we think are less vital to our survival—or to ourselves;
- hope are magical formulas for warding off tension and anxiety;
- believe to promise a moment of happiness during a demanding day;

o design to masquerade "unladylike" feelings as their
opposite;

o intend as patches on problems that we won't let
ourselves deal with now, when we are so busy or tired or
needed by others.

Fixes are also behaviors that women don't want to give up,
despite the slightly sinister sound of their name. Why not? Because fixes work. They are rewarding. They make things better.
The only problem is, they tend to make things worse in the long
run. They fail to remedy underlying problems, because they
contribute to other problems. Take, for example, the snack—a
small comfort that many women turn to. There is a moment of
pleasure as the chocolate meets the taste buds, but afterwards,
there may be *consequences*. A snack as quick pick-me-up may
lead to a low blood sugar level later; too many snacks may result
in a weight problem, which affects health and self-esteem.

At the same time, a fix can *interfere* with other areas of your
life. Suppose your fix is sleeping pills. You may find that you
pay for a good night's sleep with grogginess the next day that
puts you at less than your best.

A fix can compromise your sense of *control and choice*—
for example, when bargain hunting becomes compulsive shopping. Suddenly you can't stop shopping, even when your bank
balance is too low to pay the bills. And finally, a fix can become
destructive instead of constructive because it is *overdone*. A nap
may be just right when you are tired, but constant napping may
tell your family that you are withdrawing from family life, just
when you need them the most.

When Fixes Become Failures

Why do we continue to seek our fixes even when they have
begun to erode the quality of our lives? Why do we buy the new

house even when we know our marriage is in trouble? Why do we keep reaching for the telephone when we know we will not hear what we need to hear? Why do we keep searching through stores when our need is for more emotional fulfillment, not closet filling? Why do we give ourselves food when we want fun? Why do we clean our drawers when we need to clean up our relationships?

We probably persist because fixes function like facades. Fixes spare us from having to come face to face with realities. If we give up a fast fix, we must face a slow solution. Or we must face a problem with no solution. Or we must admit that without the fix, we feel more vulnerable or sad or frightened or resentful or dissatisfied. We might have to look at our dependencies on others, our disorganization, our human failings, and, even worse, our unmentionable strengths. If we admit to ourselves just how capable we are, would we be able to compromise our capacities to fulfill some of the roles society still dictates for us? Maybe we would. But maybe not. Fixes help us focus on the moment only and avoid such unsettling thoughts and questions.

Fixes also support many demands we make on ourselves. We can be:

- action-oriented when faced with a disaster or with free time;
- productive even when down-time would help us last for the long run;
- focused on others first, and on ourselves only after they are cared for.

These are not necessarily our chosen or conscious requirements for ourselves, but modes of behavior that are subtly taught by women to daughters and granddaughters, even by women who should know better. The "How to Have It All" school of womanhood teaches girls that they must try to be everything to everyone: mother, wife, professional, home-maker, lover, friend, commuter, carpenter, decorator, nutritionist, therapist, and bodybuilder! Build your career when you are young, have your children when you are young, plan for your retirement when you are young, take your calcium when you are young, and beware of too much sun. Keep your marriage young as you age, keep your body trim as you age, keep your career as a hedge against the empty-nest syndrome and your nest as a hedge against widowhood. Be all you can be, be all you should be, be all you might be, and all you want to be—these are the new messages.

As a clinical psychologist, I see women who seem to have all these things—job, family, money, beauty, clothes, jewelry—and yet they tell me they feel empty inside. Many of the women I interviewed for this book told me they are so busy they didn't know *what* they felt! These emotional climates are ripe for fixes, and very often concern about fixes is what sends women to me. We work together to separate the demands of society and of other people from the wants, needs, wishes, and desires of the woman herself.

Getting Yourself Back

If you have feelings like these, this book will give you insight into your behavior—and the knowledge you need to get your behavior under control!

It is time for you to slow down and remember how to relax, to be spontaneous and emotionally expansive. To slow down to a pace that permits you to deal with problems realistically and constructively, rather than do rush jobs because you expect yourself to keep going at any cost. It's time to focus on functioning well, rather than just functioning. Learn to recognize *your* fast fixes and the reasons for each. Accept your vulnerability to colds, fatigue, and headaches. We may think we want to keep going at any cost, but often the cost is too high.

M-E-N

You will also want to take a look at the men in your life. Men, women tell me, press a lot of the triggers for fixes. Here is a list of those triggers, with the most frequent ones listed first:

1. Money matters: mismanagement, miserliness, manipulations.
2. Indifference: distancing, tuning out, lip service.
3. Affairs: one-night stands, ongoing others, flirtations.
4. Drinking: abusive reactions, withdrawn reactions, hypersexual reactions.

It would be nice if I could tell you that all you need do to keep those triggers from being pushed is to get the situations under control, but that's exactly the problem: It's close to impossible to get control of a man with a huge temper, a huge opinion, or a huge desire to be with someone else. Loss of complete control is a very uncomfortable feeling but practically inevitable in some cases. So, again and again, we turn to fast fixes to increase our sense of control. Though success is sometimes only momentary and does not serve us well over time, our aim is *not* self-punishment. If we shop in reaction to feeling our spouse has a stingy soul, we are trying to declare our independence and entitlement. If we yell in the face of indifference, we are trying to confirm our ability to have an effect. If we drink or try to numb the hurt with drugs when our partner has an affair, we are not being masochistic. More likely, we are trying to quiet our feelings enough to keep our household going even though we fear he might be leaving. If we try to fix his drinking with our own, it is likely that we feel less alone when we do.

The Six Fixes

No two women I interviewed for this book had the same stories, and yours is likely to be different, too. Since you are an individual, you probably will identify with only one or two of the six kinds of fixes that women commonly turn to, because they speak of different types of inner psychology. (If you do use all six fixes, you might be in the midst of a hurricane of emotion and need professional help now.)

The six fixes are:

FOOD FIXES. Eating for you is a kind of comfort. You secretly feel that you spend too much time thinking about food. Chocolate may pop up frequently in your reveries. *Not* eating may also attract you because it feels like control.

SHOPPING FIXES. If you have any free time, you spend it in a store. You have many store charge cards, and the balances are quite high. Some months you can't cover your bills out of your checking account. It makes you feel happy to buy yourself a little gift, even if it is something you will never wear or use.

QUICK FIXES. Among the quick fixes are telephoning, redecorating, yelling, cleaning, fantasies, working too hard, TV watching, beauty makeovers. These give you instant relief that is gone within minutes or hours.

SECRET FIXES. You feel guilty about napping, masturbating, sexual gambols, and gambling, so you keep them secret from those around you.

BIG FIXES. Big fixes take only a moment to decide upon, far longer to execute. Among them are new babies, new houses, and new husbands.

FIXES THAT KILL. These life-threatening fixes are often not taken seriously enough—they may energize you or relax you, and what could be a more noble goal?—but they can indeed be fatal. They are alcohol, nicotine, caffeine, amphetamines, tranquilizers, sleeping pills, marijuana, cocaine.

Each category of fixes includes behaviors that are not necessarily problematic. They are not behaviors that must suggest depression, dependency, narcissism, chronic anger, hysteria, compulsions, or obsessions. Rather, they start as everyday behaviors that are part of our spontaneous repertoire.

Fixes That Work

Some favorite fixes that women list are just short-term fun.

"I fix my nails when I need a quick fix. Then I have the pleasure of looking at them as I work at my desk the next day."

"I redecorate my apartment. I don't mean that I buy anything new; I just rearrange everything. Then I feel like I'm visiting someone else or that I've moved."

"I clean my wallet out. I reorganize it, get rid of those receipts I don't need. When I fix up my wallet, I feel like I've fixed up my whole life—until it's bulging again. That is, my wallet, my life, and me. We all bulge!"

"I restyle my hair. The time flies and I feel like I'm all fixed up. Sometimes I leave it the new way, and sometimes I don't. But I always have fun."

9

"You may laugh at this, but my favorite fixer-upper is a list. I make a list, then love crossing items off as I get them done."

"My fix is a drive in the country. I'm lucky to live near a beautiful country road, and I drive and drive."

"Do you know any other women who watch cartoons? Not often, but once in a while on Saturday morning I sit down with my kids and have fun. It gives me a lift for hours."

"I think scary movies are my addiction. When I'm watching one, all my problems go out of my head. Sometimes I go out of my head, but then I just laugh when it's over."

"A great book is a great fix. I can take it with me wherever I go. A slow bus? More time to read before I have to get dinner!"

Behaviors like these cross the line between innocent to problematic only when they are used *excessively* or *unrealistically* or *repetitively* in order to fix a feeling. When the fix doesn't fit the situation, we should give it up. When we don't, the fix itself begins to become a problem. We feel locked into a remedy that we don't like and that is not working.

The Number-One Fast Fix

The most frequently used fast fix was absolutely clear: eating. Among married women, 55 percent of women in their twenties, 56 percent of women in their thirties, 55 percent of women in their forties, and 75 percent of women in their fifties and older said they pop food in their mouth as their quick fix for stress, fatigue, boredom, anger, depression, or frustration. Among single women, 70 percent try to munch their way to happiness. Fifty percent of divorced women and 50 percent of widowed women also list eating as a fast fix they use every day.

No other fix was used as regularly or consistently throughout all age groups and stages of life as was eating. Shopping was the second most frequently listed compulsion, but only half as many women in each group listed shopping compared to eating. What do we eat when we need a fix? The three top fixes are chocolate, chocolate, and chocolate! Chocolate candy, chocolate cookies, and chocolate anything else!

Tied for second place on the lists are other sweets and ice cream. Then another tie: junk foods and fast foods. Junk foods are stocked for "the kids" but eaten by us. Fast foods often don't make it from the take-out window to our front door. Pasta is next. Although it's on the top of my list, it's number six among the hundreds of women who were revealing their secret snacking selections. Maybe it's because a plate of pasta is harder to hide than a bar of chocolate. After pasta, it's bread, salty foods, and then general grazing through the refrigerator. There are, of course, many other favorites, but none listed frequently enough to be consensual:

"Peanut butter and jelly have been my passion since I was about five!"

"I eat pretzels all day long. I knock the salt off with my thumb, and that keeps me busy in between."

"I drink soda when I'm low. Maybe it's the bubbles, maybe it's the sugar, or maybe it's to get even with my parents who never let me drink it."

"My house is *never* without potato chips. They are the staff of life to me."

"Glazed doughnuts, powdered doughnuts, iced doughnuts —my girlfriend gave me a four-foot doughnut with candles as my birthday cake two years ago!"

The First Runner-Up

Although only half as many women listed shopping as their most frequent fix compared to eating, shopping was listed as *consistently* across age groups and marital status as eating. Between 20 and 27 percent of almost all groups shopped as a quick fix: married women in their twenties, thirties, forties, fifties, and older; single women; and widowed women. The only exception was the divorced group. They shopped more. Thirty-three percent of divorced women shopped to make themselves feel better. Some shopped by mail, some bought and returned, some shopped for others, some just browsed, some specialized in shoes or housewares or makeup, but they shopped.

Frequent Fixes

Besides shopping and eating, no other fixes are shared as consistently by the women I surveyed. Smoking, for example, was higher among younger single women (24 percent) than younger married women (15 percent). On the other hand, more older married women (23 percent) smoked than older widows (10 percent). The divorced group had the highest smoking rate of all (30 percent).

Sleeping away problems was a fix reported mainly by young married mothers (25 percent) and widows over fifty (40 percent). The first group often commented on their fatigue, and the second on their lack of evening social life.

The myth of the frustrated women scrubbing and ironing and reorganizing her closets to wear herself out seems to be just that—a myth. Twenty percent of widows and married women under forty (17 percent) do say in the survey that they often sew, clean cabinets, garden, and shine or polish when they want to unwind, but most women see these as chores, not fixes. Yelling and crying seem to be frequently used quick fixes, though not favorites. Sixteen to 18 percent of surveyed single, married, or divorced women in their twenties cry to release tension. So do 10 percent of the sample of widowed women of any age. Yelling seems to be most characteristic of married women in their thirties and forties (25 percent). A significant percent of the sample's single women say they yell as well as cry when they feel overwhelmed (20 percent), but they complain that living alone limits the number of people around to yell at. Pets and male drivers will do in a pinch, though, and Mom is available by phone . . .

Alcohol and coffee abuse were reported among younger women more frequently than older women, but national statistics suggest that "reporting" and "abusing" may be very different figures in the case of alcohol and other drugs. Although younger women indeed may be able to tolerate and therefore use more caffeine (including cola drinks), alcohol as an ageless quick fix seems to be more widespread among women than my statistics or other national statistics would reflect. Since a woman in a bar or walking around drunk seems to have a more negative connotation than a man, and since many women still function mainly in the home, where drinking as a fix can be hidden, all statistics are probably underestimates.

And what of telephoning? I certainly expected to find that we reach for the telephone for a fast fix. But I was wrong. My sample suggests we seem to reach for the telephone to say "Hello," "Goodbye," and "What's the matter?" but it's not our first impulse when we are feeling in need of a fix. Perhaps because we expect ourselves to take care of our problems by ourselves. Reaching for the telephone would be reaching out to another, being out of control, or sounding like we are complaining. Once again, the data suggest that we feel that we must be in charge and in control of making things better, quickly, quietly, and on our own.

Another World

The television—especially in its dramatic daytime form, the soap opera—is a popular fix, but the reasons are varied. For one group of women, who have been living quiet lives at home for years, TV is stimulation. On soap operas, the fashions are exciting, the faces divine, the sex steamy. The problems seem far worse than anything in a real woman's life, which makes her feel satisfied and in control. For another group of women, the soaps are restful fantasy, an escape perhaps from a long Things to Do list or a heavy course load. If you have ever watched a soap opera with a group of college girls, you probably heard hooting, sighing, and giggling!

Ideally, soap operas should be taken in moderation, but how can they be? They are designed to be addictive. The hour often closes with a cliffhanger of an ending: a woman making the phone call that will tell her if she is pregnant or not, a car poised on a precipice, a child about to learn the identity of her real father. Who could fail to tune in the next day to find out what happens?

If watching TV goes beyond entertainment to become an obsession—if you watch for hours, if it prevents you from doing other things, if you feel anxious when you miss a show—it is time to examine the reasons you feel you need to enter another world. Breaking a TV habit takes self-examination: Is life boring? Is sex boring? Are TV characters substitutes for real friends?

Patterns and Profiles

Finding patterns of fixes is important since it helps us predict what we may do next. But don't confuse correlations with cause-and-effect relationships. Just because two behaviors are likely to be associated, follow each other, or precede each other does not mean that they cause each other. Take crying and yelling. A tired child may do both, but the crying didn't cause the yelling, or vice versa. A third factor, fatigue, made both behaviors more likely.

Now let's examine our fixes. Eating and shopping fixes are significantly related in this study. That means the two behaviors are associated far more often than we could expect by chance alone. If you secretly snack, you are very likely also to dash into available stores when you have an extra ten minutes. Likewise, if you dash into stores, you are likely to dash into the refrigerator for fixes as well. They are both taking-in type behaviors.

The Taking-In Fixes

A woman who needs something—love, attention, recognition —may reach for one of the taking-in fixes. They are both ways in which we can give to ourselves.

Whenever Marie knew a weekend without a date was coming up, she stocked up. Chips, dips, pasta, and pastries kept her company. She sweetened up her weekend and made herself feel cared for with food. She mingled her eating with quick trips to stores for necessities. She bought herself gadgets at the hardware store, desk things at the card shop, and the newest face creams at the pharmacy. Sometimes

15

she would take in a movie, too. She would order an oldie from the video store and feel fine Saturday night.

By Sunday morning, her acquisitions would begin again. She'd take in brunch, bargains, and paperback books to get through the day.

Taking-in fixes often do not have staying power. By the end of a session your wallet is emptier and you feel no fuller.

Not only do the women who participated in this survey use shopping and eating as fixes more frequently and consistently than any other behaviors, but if they do one, there is a 40 percent chance that they also do the other. Some women say that they alternate these ways of giving to themselves. Some say that as their eating goes up, their shopping goes down. "After all," one respondent said, "who wants to look in a dressing-room mirror when you've just put on eleven pounds?" Others say that as their feelings of neediness climb, so does their food *and* goods consumption: "Whether it's a housewares store, a clotheswear store, or a candy store, I do heavy damage when I'm feeling that I've got to fix up my feelings to go on."

If taking-in behaviors are the most frequent and most highly correlated of the female fixes, does this suggest that we may be "giving out" to others more than is good for us? In a very general way, the answer is "probably." If we expend energy and effort because of the satisfaction we get by doing so, our sense of choice and control is usually not diminished. My research on the female stress syndrome clearly indicated that when we give to others in order to get permission to rest or relax, we never get back enough and what we do get is too small a comfort. Since our agenda is usually hidden, others come to learn what we seem to be teaching them: that we can do it all, and more. We keep turning to quick fixes, secret fixes, or big fixes to keep going. We ourselves must set our own limits, be realistic, decide to rest, relax, and play before we are incapacitated by mental or physical exhaustion. *We ourselves must have a sense of choice and control over our giving-out and our taking-in behaviors in order to free ourselves from fixes that do not fix!*

The Letting-It-Out Fixes

Although it was popular in the sixties to give a primal scream, share your private thoughts, and tell it like it was, research has found that most uncontrolled cathartic behavior serves only as practice for more of the same. Yelling and excessive sex are two examples of this type of quick fix. Yell at someone to make yourself feel better, and you will probably get some yelling in return. Then you have an excuse to yell some more. The original problem is temporarily obscured in a barrage of escalating anger. Sex as a secret fix can work the same way:

> Val felt like flirting whenever she was feeling numb. She would go beyond fun and try to see how far she would go with a stranger before she would say "no." She'd say whatever came to her mind and dress as revealingly as she dared. For a short time she'd feel as if she was alive and open and showing it all to the world, but only for a short time. The next morning she would again feel numb, as though her feelings were blocked from flowing.

The problem with pouring out emotions with abandon is that it often creates more problems than it solves. And more than likely, the feelings come from an infinite reserve!

Distractions

With distractions, we make our problems seem smaller by taking on bigger ones! We buy a new house, or have a baby just when we are feeling more worried than we have in years:

17

Helene had felt lonely ever since Robert bought his boat. She couldn't kayak with him since she was terrified of the water, but he bought it anyway and plunged into courses and outings. She kept telling herself that married people should have separate interests, and she still questioned whether his boating wasn't *too* separate. She wanted the marriage to go on, so she did not challenge his behavior. She decided that a baby would fix up all their problems. She'd no longer be lonely, and Robert would want to stay home and play with the baby. Things didn't work quite that way. Helene and the baby were now home alone on weekends. For a few years, she didn't care as much. For a few years . . .

With this kind of big fix, dissatisfaction first yields to satisfaction and possibly even to great joy. However, the solution is superficial, and eventually the dissatisfaction returns and may become unmanageable.

Use-It-Up-Behaviors

If extra adrenaline has flowed all day while you were stuck in gridlock, use it up. If you feel that you have a lot of running and jumping inside because you were chained to a desk all day, use it up. Cleaning and exercise are use-it-up fixes. When do cleaning and exercising become problems? When you no longer feel that you have a choice about them. When they become compulsive and begin to control you. When your fix begins to have a life of its own!

Debbie looked younger than she felt. Debbie *was* younger than she felt. She had just turned thirty, but had no energy in the evenings. Her doctor's diagnosis? All work and not enough play. She warned Debbie that her daily fast-track race was keeping her heart and head running, but not burning up tension. A jog around the park after work would get Debbie into the fresh air, away from her desk, and help her meet new people too. Debbie loved the idea and tried it.

For a few months, Debbie found running in the park to be relaxing and energizing. She was less likely to munch in the evening and more likely to sleep from being tired than to toss from being fatigued. But within six months Debbie was back in her doctor's office. She now ran so much that she had stopped menstruating and had lost too much weight. The remedy for fatigue had become an addiction. Debbie had found a new fast track—and a new problem!

Some women use the adrenaline they've produced during a wild day at the office to *stay* at the office and work some more! It's called workaholism, and it's a special temptation for the woman who feels she has little control. She may work late in a struggle to regain control over a job that has gotten away from her during the day, or she may enjoy staying late because she has more control in the office than she does at home. Being at work is also a way of not being somewhere else.

Observing our own behavior and being aware of when it crosses the line from healthy pursuit to unhealthy obsession is difficult—we ourselves are often the last to know! If you suspect your behavior is excessive, look into it. Don't brush off your suspicion. And listen to other people. Although it's important not to let others run your life for you, they can be sources of important information about you.

Self-Medication

As I examine women's use of nicotine, caffeine, alcohol, co-caine, tranquilizers, and sleeping pills, I find that the majority of women are taking these drugs in an attempt to function better. They are *not* trying to hurt or destroy their daily life, but are trying to make it run more smoothly. If they are down, they reach for uppers. If they are too uptight, they reach for downs. If they are upset, they reach for tranquilizers. If they are turned off, they turn on. Self-medication is dangerous, often addictive, and doomed to failure. But we must keep in mind that the aim of women using these fixes is to try to behave in a way they think is "normal."

> Kelly was frightened because she was becoming indifferent to sex with her husband. They had been married three years and she still loved him, but she wanted to sleep when they got into bed. Her job, the baby, his mother—it was all too much. On their ski vacation, a friend offered them some marijuana. It had been years since they had used it, but that night Kelly tried it again. She was not sure whether she enjoyed sex more, objected less, or was mainly reacting to her husband's enthusiasm, but sex was okay again.
>
> After that night, Kelly was afraid to try sex without marijuana. They eventually needed both sex therapy and drug counseling to fix their need for a fix.

"Drug counseling"—it is an expression we hear so often that it has lost its impact. Drug use is so common that we forget how dangerous it can be. As any teenager who sees the "Rock Against Drugs" advertisements knows, drugs can kill, even the ones like marijuana that seem innocuous—they can lead to auto accidents, for example, and possibly long-term health consequences that are easy not to think about when you are remedying a problem that exists now. Self-medication is a small comfort that can mean big trouble.

The Fast Track

Although I expected many more clusters of correlated fixes, I did not find them. Eating fixes were generally associated with yelling and sleeping fixes, and smoking was generally associated with cleaning compulsions, but these co-relationships (correlations) were not much higher than we would expect to get between any two fixes by chance alone. Much to my surprise, particular fixes did appear to be more related to the personality characteristics of women than they were to each other. In particular, "fast pace" personality characteristics related to "fast fix" patterns.

There are a set of fourteen characteristics that I label "fast pace"—tendencies that significantly increase our risk of reaching for fixes. These characteristics keep our autonomic nervous system on "emergency" speed. They keep the adrenaline flowing. They mean that whether we are working full time at home, full time on the job, or full time at both, we drive ourselves until we feel all used up.

Our desire for a sense of control often interferes with an objective look at just how much we are overloading ourselves. There is no better way to be objective than to put pencil to paper, tote up your score, and see the results in black and white. To see if you know yourself as well as you think you do, check your score on what I call the Fast Pace Profile for Women.

The Fast Pace Profile for Women

0 points = never true
1 point = sometimes true
2 points = usually true

1. _____ When the telephone rings, I assume it's a new demand, emergency, or problem for me to deal with.

2. _____ When someone is in a bad mood around the house or office, I ask myself if I might have done something to upset them.

3. _____ Even if I find out that I have not upset someone but that they are indeed upset, I feel I must make them feel better.

4. _____ I overschedule myself, leaving no time for unexpected delays or emergencies.

5. _____ I make all my roles equal priorities and feel guilty if one suffers because of the demands of another.

6. _____ Criticism has a powerful effect on me, so I criticize myself to beat everyone else to the punch.

7. _____ I create busywork because I get more done when I have more to do.

8. _____ I know exactly how I like things to be done and try to do them that way.

9. _____ I get upset when others don't do things as well or as fast as I do them.

10. _____ Even when I get upset that others are not performing as well as I could, I try to keep my feelings secret.

11. _____ I do more than I should rather than delegate

responsibility or worry about how well a job will be done.

12. _____ I feel like I am wasting time if I don't do more than one thing at a time, like opening the mail while I eat lunch *and* talk on the telephone.

13. _____ I do things the hard way so that I have a good excuse in case I fail.

14. _____ I hate to wait!

Add up your score and divide by 2.

0–3 points: Even a score of 1 point puts you on the fast track to fast fixes! But at this level, you are not likely to be needing fixes now.

4–7 points: You are already running a daily race with yourself. Data shows you are having trouble keeping up.

8–10 points: You are in the group which is at highest risk for fast fixes! You must try to moderate the demands you put on yourself and others.

11–14 points: Although you seem to be personalizing others' behavior and perfecting your own, you have probably set up your outlets and intakes enough to survive—but not thrive. It is time to try to bring your score down by reexamining your expectations of yourself and others.

Fast Pace, Fast Fix?

The commonsense prediction would be that as a woman's Fast Pace score climbed, so would her use of fast fixes. The more energy she put out, the more she would need to take in. The more tension she generated, the more she would need to let it out. The more worrying and obsessing she did, the more distraction she would need. But, in fact, that is not the way fast fixes and fast paces related. Look at fast fix eating, for example.

EATING

```
percent using
food as a fix
  50
  45                                      x
  40                      x   x           x
  35                      x   x           x
  30                  x   x   x   x   x   x           x
  25              x   x   x   x   x   x   x   x   x
  20              x   x   x   x   x   x   x   x   x
  15              x   x   x   x   x   x   x   x   x   x
  10              x   x   x   x   x   x   x   x   x   x   x
   5      x   x   x   x   x   x   x   x   x   x   x   x   x   x
   0      x   x   x   x   x   x   x   x   x   x   x   x   x   x
Fast Pace Score:  1   2   3   4   5   6   7   8   9  10  11  12  13  14  points
```

Except for a peak for women who scored 10 on the Fast Pace Scale, the general pattern is that both ends of the scale reach for snacks and food fixes *less* frequently than women who are in the mid-range! This suggests good news and bad news. The good news is that the less we push ourselves to be ideal rather than real, the less we seem to need to fill ourselves with food to keep going. The bad news seems to be that women can become so fast-paced, overscheduled, and overloaded that they are probably too tense or too overwrought to be able to snack, take food breaks, or even eat properly.

This graph is not the only factor that leads me to make the suggestion that women who become exceptionally stressed find that they are beyond the temporary help that quick food fixes provide. Ulcers and digestive problems have long been a hallmark of the high-powered, competitive male; now physicians are seeing an increase among women. *Anorexia* (loss of appetite) has long been a female stress sign as well as a sign of depression. Some of the women in the high-scoring group tell me, "I just *forget* to eat when I'm preoccupied and pressed for time."

Shopping, the second most frequently used fix, shows a pattern that is the inverse of eating!

SHOPPING

```
percent using
shopping as a fix
   50
   45
   40
   35
   30
   25              x
   20              x       x x x              x
   15              x x x x x                  x
   10              x x x x x           x  x  x
    5              x x x x x           x  x  x
    1        *  *  *  x x x x x x x   x  x  x   *
Fast Pace Score: 1  2  3  4 5 6 7 8 9 10 11 12 13 14  points
```

* No data.

Although shopping and eating overlap for almost half of the women surveyed, for the group of women who scored 9 or 10, eating takes precedence. Women scoring 9 and 10 points on the Fast Pace Scale might well be those women who are busiest as homemakers, with greater access to the refrigerator than to the shopping malls. Those women who score even higher may be women who have older children or are earning more and spending more outside the home.

The important point is that every woman seems to have her own personality profile and her own pattern of fixes. General patterns, then, can help only in general predictions. Yelling, for example, seems to pick up just where shopping leaves off. Women scoring 9, 10, and 11 points on the Fast Pace Scale seem to do the most yelling and the most eating and the least shopping. It is very important to note that one third of the more than 1,000 women taking this profile scored 9, 10, and 11 points. So let's see what else is typical for this group in general.

- More crying than lower or higher groups.
- More smoking than lower or higher groups.
- More telephone talking.
- More napping and early bedtime.

As one woman in this group wrote to me, "I eat starches and sweets, cry, fight, get on the phone and yell for help. No one understands me! I push myself and others around me. I'm learning that nothing is perfect—but I still find I try to make things that way."

Another woman explains why eating and yelling may drop off the charts for the very highly paced and self-demanding woman: "I find that I eat especially when I'm angry. As though I was stuffing the anger down so it wouldn't come out. But then it builds to a point that I can't stuff it down anymore. Then I stop eating and *do* something about it!"

Another woman added, "When things get bad enough, I just shut down and shut out everything. Then there are no fixes for a while."

So now you know the surveyed women's favorite fixes: food and shopping. You know that all the fixes fall into groups: quick, secret, big, fatal. Do you know what is behind them all?

TWO

What Needs Fixing?

Ask *many* women the question, "What needs fixing?" and they will answer, "Everything!" Ask *most* women the question, and they can be more specific: depression, demands, guilt, anger, low self-esteem, aging, and boredom. The list does not stop here, but these answers are the most frequent. Does "boredom" surprise you? Do you feel that you would welcome boredom after your typical day? Boredom means many things to different people. Some women referred to boredom as a routine that had rusted over the years. Others meant that hour on Sunday that was left unscheduled. Still others missed their children or husband and felt bored caring only for themselves.

In addition to these feelings that women try to fix for themselves, they also list traumas. Traumas are life events that may make us feel a bit broken or very broken indeed. A trauma might be an undesired relocation ordered by your head office. You make the move, but your smoking increases with every day that you spend packing. A trauma might be an unexpected romantic breakup. He walks out, and you start ordering food in. Fixing traumas and emotions is a demanding task, particularly when we are trained to help others before we help ourselves.

There is yet one more fix-it project we need to consider. If you scored even one point on the Fast Pace Profile, then some of your attitudes probably need changing too. The Fast Pace Profile tells us that we are not unlike the Type A man described by Dr. Meyer Friedman and Dr. Ray Rosenman over a decade ago in their book *Type A Behavior and Your Heart*. Their hypothesis was that chronic competitiveness, chronic anger, and chronic hurrying was predisposing men to heart attacks. Their research has supported a link between chronic anger and heart attacks. Behavior modification seems to decrease the risk of a second heart attack.

The Type A Profile test does not fit women well for two reasons. Our competitiveness, demanding quality, and high self-expectations manifest differently than in men, who were trained to compete openly, take charge, and relax after work. Furthermore, we are not as high risk before menopause for heart attacks under pressure, but rather for anxiety attacks, depression, headaches, and eating disturbances instead. In other words, measure yourself on the Fast Pace Profile for Women as a man would measure himself on the Type A Behavior Scale. The higher your score on the Women's Fast Pace Profile, the more likely that you are adding to life's traumas and pushing yourself toward quick fixes, secret fixes, big fixes, or fixes that kill. A first step toward giving up our need for fixes is to understand the feelings and traumas they are aimed at.

Feelings That Need Fixing

Depression, despair, and other downs:

"I feel low, a lot. Not depressed, not suicidal; just low."

"When I start crying about a house plant turning brown, I know I'm in trouble. If I'm not premenstrual, then I'm depressed!"

"I live alone and love to stay home. But sometimes it does lead me to feel like I'm shut out of the world, and I get sad."

"Some days everyone is unfriendly. Even the bus driver seems to be picking me to yell at. I just want to give up."

Does this sound like depression? Most women list depression as a feeling they are often trying to fix, but more often they are really feeling despair. Compare the two feelings in order to understand yourself better:

When we give up on ourselves because we feel we are not worth much, that is *depression*.

When we give up on the world because we feel that life is not worth much, that is *despair*.

If we are having trouble falling asleep or are waking at the crack of dawn, that is *depression*.

If we find that all we want to do is crawl into bed and sleep the hours away, that is *despair*.

When we brood and "awfulize" all day and are tormented by unrealistic worries all night, that is *depression*.

When we find that our mood darkens in the evening as the sky darkens, that is *despair*.

If we feel helpless and to blame for our own misery, that is *depression*.

If we feel hopeless as if the world let us down, that is *despair*.

Although women seem to have a higher risk of depression than men, we too often label our despair as depression. If we are indeed depressed, then professional consultation is important because depression is an illness. Self-help books and talk shows will not fix your problem. Even if it passes, seek help so that you can prevent it from reoccurring. Use the guidelines above to determine if you are really depressed, and ask yourself the following questions also:

1. Have you lost pleasure in almost all activities?
2. Have you lost a significant amount of weight without dieting?
3. Are you feeling excessive guilt?
4. Is it hard for you to concentrate lately?
5. Have you lost your achievement drive or sex drive?
6. Have you withdrawn socially?
7. Do you feel slowed down and less productive?
8. Do you feel continually pessimistic about the future or brood about the past?
9. Are you tearful or crying frequently?
10. Are you excessively irritable or angry?

Taken from the American Psychiatric Association's guidelines for depression, *three* or more "yes" responses to these questions suggests that you are depressed. Start by seeing your physician to rule out anemia, viral aftermath, drug side effects, nutritional deficiencies (particularly B_1, B_6, and B_{12}), central nervous system disorders, hormonal disorders, or chronic pain syndrome. Take a hard look at your own drug use: Is it abuse? Once these factors are ruled out, let your physician refer you to a psychiatrist (M.D.), a state-licensed clinical psychologist (Ph.D.), or a certified social worker (C.S.W.) for a diagnosis.

If your response to most of these questions is "Only sometimes," or "Rarely," or, "Once in a while for a brief time," you are probably not depressed but are in and out of despair.

How Despair Begins

Despair can become depression, but it is more often a temporary state triggered by events outside of us: being passed over for a promotion, finding the basement flooded, finding a goodbye note from a new lover or old husband, having to get used to crutches after a sprain, or dealing with your child's drug problem.

Although despair is a powerful mind–body emotion, we feel whole and healthy again when despair passes. If a not-so-temporary fix has been introduced to the problem, we can be left with a new problem to deal with after the problem and despair have passed. The experiences that follow illustrate my point:

"I couldn't conceive a child, and I was getting desperate. My husband checked out fine and so did I, but nothing was happening. I began to eat. I think it made me feel less empty. I certainly began to look pregnant! When I finally became pregnant, I was twenty pounds overweight."

"I decided that Dennis and I could never work things out. We started separation proceedings and he moved out. I was afraid to be alone and quickly got involved with an old boyfriend who was still interested in me. I let him move in because the house seemed so empty. Within a month I wanted to work things out with Dennis, but now I didn't know what to do about my housemate."

"My husband was fired unexpectedly. My job didn't cover the expenses. I couldn't sleep! I started drinking some wine before bed. It helped me sleep. Soon I was drinking just in case I might not be able to sleep. By the time John was working again, I couldn't sleep without drinking."

Women are susceptible to despair for the same reasons that they are likely to reach out to fixes. We have learned to different degrees that the outside world may be more powerful than our inside world. That both disaster and help come from without, not within. We are raised, typically, in a more protected way than boys, suggesting to us that we need more protection. We are raised, typically, in a more gentle way, suggesting to us that we might lose in competition. We learn to be approval junkies, so that failure means more than our own disappointment—it means shame. We learn that appearing to be cooperative will get us further than appearing to be assertive or decisive.

What of the "new woman" we try to be? In a study I completed for *Health* Magazine (November 1984), I found that women who identified themselves as "new women" felt that they had to deal with more real-world disappointments than men:

- She is usually paid less than a man in the same job.
- She is accused often of being emotional when she shows strong feelings.
- She feels that her aging works against her in the marketplace and social arena more than her experience counts for her.
- She knows that despite her best efforts, she is more likely to end up alone than a man, through divorce, widowhood, or lack of available partners.

Three-Step Despair Management

How can we better survive despair without reaching for a quick fix, secret fix, big fix, or fix that may eventually kill us? Fix your focus, instead. Don't focus on the trauma of the moment, but rather focus on these three real changes you can make in time:

1. **When you are feeling ineffective, practice decision-making skills.** Make choices about that evening, that weekend, or

that lunch hour, as a beginning. Take all choices that are offered to you. If a friend suggests that you pick up a movie, don't say, "I don't care, it's up to you." Take the choice even if you don't care! It's good practice. You will feel more in control. Even if the movie turns out to be terrible, you will see that the consequences of taking a choice and taking control are not disastrous—just sometimes disappointing. Finally, create choices for yourself. Even on trivial things. Deciding to try a new type of hobby beats trying a new drug or bar.

2. **When you are feeling down because of the way you think the world sees you, switch your focus to how you see the world and how you see yourself.** You might feel angry when you take a clear look around you at the people you work with or play with, but better to feel angry than anxious. You might think you know how everyone sees you, but you are probably somewhat off base. If you are really concerned, ask. Or stick with how you see yourself and you see them. It's less draining than trying to read your mind and theirs, too! Fixing your focus on how you see the world and others is better than a quick fix that fades fast.

3. **When an accident, illness, death, disappointment, or disaster hits you hard, remind yourself that you are not being punished.** Even though we logically know that life is a package deal and that there will always be sad and frustrating events over which we have no control, women too often think that they have lost control. The reality is that we sometimes don't have control. To struggle against reality is futile. It uses up our energy and leads us to temporary fixes. In situations beyond your control, let time be your fix. Despair can be a stage of readjustment, a mourning period, an anger period, or a tired period. After despair, life will look a little different, more

33

textured perhaps. With fast fixes, it will only look more complicated.

Rage Reactions

Anger is another feeling that women may try to quick-fix rather than work out or work through. *Working out* anger usually involves two: the source of your anger and you. *Working through* anger usually takes time: the time to cool off and the time to move on. If you feel that you must fix your feeling this minute, you are likely to reach for a fast fix and be left with the consequences of both your anger and the fix!

We commonly feel *rage* at the onset of anger. Since rage involves the body's fight-and-flight system, we are pushed toward immediate action. If we choose to fight, we may yell, throw, even hit. If we choose flight, we may slam doors, leave the house, or threaten to leave. Adrenaline pours into our bloodstream and stimulates our heart rate, respiration, and release of stored sugars for energy. What we do in rage is done under the influence of our own stimulant "drug," adrenaline. According to Albert Bandura, Ph.D., in his book *Aggression*, what we say afterwards is "It wasn't my fault." In fact, here are nine ways we may try to say, "It wasn't my fault":

o What I did wasn't as bad as what I might have done.
o I didn't start it.
o The way I behaved was wrong, but it worked.
o They deserved it.
o He/she isn't worth bothering with, so it doesn't matter.
o I only behaved the way he/she did.
o Everyone does the same thing.
o I warned them but they didn't listen.
o It's healthy to let the anger out.

Is it really healthier to let the anger out? Research tells us that neither holding in anger nor exploding with rage is healthy. Although the rage reaction probably served us well in the wild, civilizations require that we channel our rage constructively. Exploding does not usually fit well into our work or family system. Furthermore, rage usually rehearses us for more rage and gives everyone else a model for rage and permission to act out also.

If we do not explode, what do we do with rage and anger instead? Probably the wrong things. Women are usually so uncomfortable with our negative impulses that we try to hide our feelings. This creates new problems. First, we miss chances to defuse infuriating situations before they reach the boiling point. Second, the angry woman turns out to be even better at hiding her feelings from herself than from anyone else. Everyone knows something is bothering her, but nobody can guess what it is! Third, the unrecognized rage can push us toward a fast fix: a drink, a tranquilizer, a snack, an affair, or a shopping spree.

Did the nine excuses sound familiar to you? Do you often convince yourself that you were not responsible for your outburst, or that it was better for you to let it all hang out? Did you ever avoid examining your aggression by saying that the victim "deserved" it? Women should be particularly sensitive to this excuse since it has been used against us for so long!

Secret Angers

If the excuses are not familiar to you, that is not necessarily good news. It could mean that you deal with anger by distorting it into depression, projection, or displacement. Although each of these defenses against anger may be your way of protecting your world from your rage, they don't protect you from the effects of inner anger.

DEPRESSION An effective anti-anger maneuver. When depressed, nothing matters enough to get angry about. Helen's case is a dramatic example:

Helen's roommate got married—to Helen's boss. Though she tried to be happy for them, she found herself too fatigued to set up a bridal shower and too disinterested to help her arrange the wedding. She spent many weeks eating in front of the television while her roommate was out at engagement events, then crawling off to bed exhausted, before she realized that she was furious at being left behind. Left behind, alone, in the apartment. And left behind socially as her friend joined her boss's social circle!

Turning anger inward, as Helen did, means keeping our anger secret—from ourselves as well as others. Soon we may feel depressed and listless since so much of our psychological energy is being used up by our attempt to hold down our potential expression of anger. Check out your own depressions for secret angers. If you find a feeling of rage beneath your depression, don't depress it or deny it. It will not go away until you deal with it.

PROJECTION This works differently. Through projection, our own unacceptable impulses become someone else's impulses. For example, if we were raised to believe that females should never show direct anger, we project our anger onto others. We see others starting fights with us. We get to feel nonaggressive by comparison. We get to be the victim rather than the instigator. We get to have our fight, without having to admit that we wanted it!

Sheryl had a hard day. The car took too long to start and the battery was too low to work the air conditioner. Caught in a traffic jam, she was very late for the office. The day was riddled with emergencies. On returning home, she found the driveway an obstacle course of bikes and toys. She wanted to yell, but she felt guilty at the mere thought of taking out her feelings on her husband. Instead, she tried to smile as she entered the door. But the minute she saw her husband, she hissed, "I know that look. You want to know why dinner is late. Well, fix your own!" An innocent and confused husband watched Sheryl slam indignantly into the bedroom.

If Sheryl had been aware of her maneuver, we could accuse her of being manipulative. But the key to projection is that it works automatically, unconsciously. And leaves us with our original problem: anger, plus the new one our projection created.

DISPLACEMENT This is a defense against our own unacceptable anger by unconsciously redirecting our fury from one person to another—an innocent person, an object, or even ourselves.

Jill had been waiting all day for her test results. After two promises that the doctor would return her call, the office closed. Now she would have to wait until tomorrow. If she called the emergency number, the doctor would probably answer from home—without the test results handy. Yelling at the nurses tomorrow would be too late. She had to release that anger immediately. So she yelled at her son instead. Then she threw the cat out of the house—it was shedding all over the sofa again—and fumed when she cut herself cleaning carrots for dinner.

We so often hurt ourselves when we displace our anger that I suspect we must be letting out some aggression and guilt about aggression in the process. But it is not going to fix our anger to

37

hurt ourselves or the innocent in an attempt to keep our real feelings secret. In fact, that is what is wrong with using these face-saving or defensive tactics. The anger is never directly confronted by us. Maybe we let off some steam, but the core of rage is still within us. Maybe we avoid some guilt about seeming a wicked witch, but the anger still seeps out. When the feelings inside go unfixed, the woman may reach for an external fix. And then we start double trouble.

What's better than defense mechanisms and fast fixes?

o **WAITING**   Act, don't react. Before you do anything, review the real cause of your rage for a few minutes. Now decide what would make you feel better and ask for it. Accusations and lashing out lead only to defensive retaliations. Specific requests can prevent your rage from returning again and again. So count to ten—and then ten again, before you shower the world with your anger. A calming delay will also help you regain a sense of control just when you are feeling most out of control.

o **COMMUNICATION**   Neither lashing out physically or verbally, nor withdrawing physically or verbally, does as much to dissipate anger as communication. Physical violence usually leads to more of the same. Yelling provokes more yelling or defensiveness. Verbal freezing leads to one-sided, imaginary conversations with no end. And physical withdrawal deprives you and your mate of the closeness that can help you both through periods of anger.

Don't bring your anger into the bedroom or dining room. Keep your focus specific to the current issue and don't let it grow. Talk out or write out your feelings and then review your own feelings objectively. An apology, a request for an explanation, or a revised letter is preferable to a discarded relationship or a fix that doesn't touch your anger.

o **ACTIVATION**   Do you remember your grandmother "furiously" cleaning the kitchen floor as she mumbled angrily under her breath? Or hummed through clenched teeth? Or scolded the freezer for needing a defrosting so often? Since rage produces adrenaline that needs to be used up, find an immediate constructive activity to substitute for a destructive anger response over which you have no immediate perspective. Move furniture, polish jewelry, clean closets, play tennis, scrub fingermarks off the walls to use up that extra adrenaline.

Remember, since the body can produce only so much adrenaline before exhaustion sets in, rage always passes. When the rage passes, you will be able to come up with practical solutions.

Recognize Chronic Anger

If your anger never seems to pass, then examine your inner and outer life carefully. Are your life circumstances really so difficult? If so, call in friends, relatives, social services, or professionals to help you set up your circumstances differently. If your life is not as provocative as your feelings would warrant, join a therapy group, counseling group, or individual therapy to sort out the real source of your anger. Snacking, sleeping, yelling, shopping, drinking, and drugs will not give you the answers you really need and deserve to have. Take the time to sort out your feelings now. It may save you years in the future if your anger is related to your past.

Old angers tend to reappear in new forms again and again until they are finally put to rest. In fact, we often recreate old situations that make us angry in order to create new outcomes. When we fail, we have compounded our anger. If you suspect you are in this chronic anger trap, let a professional help you out of it.

The Guilt Trap

In my survey, *guilt* was consistently listed as one of the emotions that give women trouble. It is almost as if a "guilt plague" has hit American womanhood. We seem to feel guilty when we don't do everything we think we should do, as well as when we do the things we think we shouldn't do. We reach for fast fixes when we feel guilty and then feel guilty about having reached for a fast fix. We are caught in a guilt trap.

Like laughter and tears, feelings of guilt are part of an inborn capacity. Most developmental psychologists estimate that this capacity emerges at around three years of age. The "terrible" two-year-old is dangerous because she does not yet have inner controls over her anger at her baby sister or puppy dog, but the three-year-old is safer because her guilt capacity is emerging. She looks around her world to find out what she should feel guilty about, and learns from those around her— her mother, babysitter, father, brothers and sisters, and other family. If she is told that good girls don't cry, yell, sulk, or fight, she will attach her guilt feelings to those impulses to cry, yell, sulk, or fight, which she feels regularly. If she is taught that "big girls" don't have those emotions at all, the age of nightmares and day fears begins. Her own angry impulses will make her so guilty that she will fear herself and dwell on monsters and demons—outer projections of inner impulses.

At best, guilt can help us control our unacceptable impulses and destructive urges. At worst, guilt can make us hide the very existence of normal, inevitable feelings from ourselves. Guilt stops four-year-olds from drawing on walls and flushing provocative pets down the toilet. For an adult, who is not likely to do either, guilt is usually superfluous. Our common sense and knowledge of the consequences of our actions is usually enough to keep us on the straight-and-narrow path—often too straight and narrow. Once we are adults, we rarely have the time, let alone the inclination, to be "bad." Once we are working women, devoted mothers, loving wives, dutiful daughters, faithful friends, and good neighbors, being bad is not even an issue. Being on time is all we can handle.

Being "bad" is not the only guilt issue. Women don't only feel guilt when they are bad. More often, they feel guilt when they are not sufficiently good. This type of guilt gets us into trouble. If we are not as good as we think we should be, and as good as we think everyone else is, we feel bad. Our self-esteem drops. Then we reach for the fast fix-me-up. Since most fast fixes are self-indulgences, we now begin to feel even worse. Our low self-esteem has just been confirmed. Why not reach for another fast fix, we think. There is no hope for us anyway.

And then come the demands—the real demands we can't ignore. Parenting our parents as they age. Receiving the call from school when our child is sick. Preparing the extra report at work to prove that we can be pregnant and still work well on the job. Hosting the family club meeting when our sister's husband has been fired and it was her turn.

The demands are real. But the guilt we feel if we decide to say no, if we don't do it all as well as our mother seemed to have done it, or if we do it but feel resentful—that guilt is not realistic. That guilt should not be associated with "bad" or "good." That guilt serves no adult purpose of any use to us.

Try to make use of the following approaches, which many therapists use with their patients who suffer from guilt. Jot the suggestions down on an index card, perhaps, and tape the card to your bathroom mirror or car dashboard as a memo to yourself. It will take time to change your guilt habit, so be patient and persistent.

o Substitute realistic for excessive expectations of yourself.
o Practice recognizing your guilty reaction when you are intentionally hurtful to yourself or another—and then figure out why you behaved that way. *Use* the information, rather than feeling guilty.
o Get to know your faults. They are as much a part of you as your strengths. Instead of blaming yourself for your faults, work with them, or around them, to try to improve them. But don't try to fast-fix them!
o Review the "good" and "bad" girl messages you received when you were very young. How many of them apply today? Does "Don't step in the puddle" apply? Since most of the old messages *don't* apply, make up your own list of messages now. A list of "wants," not "shoulds." A list built on choice, not guilt!

Aging, Fixes, and Frustrations

Last but not least, women often feel their age is a problem for them. This response is not vanity talking. It is the reality of the eighties that women are more valuable socially and in the workplace if they are perceived as healthy and young enough to provide many years of "service."

Though many women find that their lives flow easily into middle age and later life, still more tell me that they cannot reconcile their years with their inner feelings. They feel ready to start a family when they find they are too old for even "older men." They feel ready to begin a new dance when they find they have disorders or diseases that make it difficult even to walk. Some feel old when they are in their late twenties and not yet married; others when they are thirty and not yet mothers; still others in their forties when they are unexpectedly single again or still single. Some must cope with problems of income, health, housing, transportation, and nutrition as they age. Some have memory, visual, hearing, or pain problems. Some women feel old at thirty, others feel young at seventy. But all women feel the double standard of aging at some point in their lives.

"I don't mind that men marry younger women. I just wish we had enough younger men to go around."

"Why do I look wrinkled while my husband looks mature?"

"Who decided that thin thighs are sexy? No men have them!"

Our age concerns surface throughout this book and throughout my research data. Younger women seem to want the sophistication that comes of age, and older women want the blush of health that is associated with youth. In terms of make-overs, this means that younger women will be hollowing out their cheekbones, and older women will be making them look round and rosy. Younger women will be putting frosted streaks in their hair, the older women will be dying their hair a deep, rich color. Younger women will be darkening their eyebrows Madonna-style, and older women will be plucking them to look delicate. Younger women will want a heavy-lidded look (perhaps purple or blue), and older women will be asking plastic surgeons to remove excess lid so they can look wide-eyed again. The younger woman will flaunt their artifice, and the older woman will try to look natural.

Since it's youthful appearance that this culture seems to use to sell every product except antacids and analgesics, it's the youthful appearance that most of us assume we will see in the mirror. When the vision in the mirror doesn't match the vision of television and magazine covers, many of us are literally surprised—because we *feel* as young as the All-American beauty. Unfortunately, the "youthful look," with lots of collagen beneath the epidermis and lots of pink on the lips and cheeks, lasts only about two decades, while we live at least seven! So most women are trying to fix their aging with magic makeovers.

Not only do we spend money, but we spend time on our remakes and do-overs. Over our life, most of us spend 3,000 hours applying makeup, washing away our natural oils and scents and then applying moisturizers and perfumes, plucking our eyebrows, shaving our legs, and perming or straightening or setting our hair. What are we trying to fix? Working from the outside in, we seem to be trying to fix our age concerns, our emotional scars, and our sex appeal.

Covering emotional scars with makeovers is more difficult than trying for the youthful look. Not only are the lines and wrinkles firmly etched as the years go by, but our expressions slip into pouts and pinches when we are tense and not monitoring ourselves.

Roberta is a buyer at a large department store. Although she has read that women are allowed to be emotional compared to men, she has found that emotions do not work on the job! If she is sad, she is treated like a child by her male counterparts. So she uses makeup to cover the puffed lids, and eyedrops to hide signs of crying. If she is depressed, she uses extra blush and brighter lipstick to look energized. If she is agitated, she uses extra perfume, so a scent rather than an anger aura precedes her!

Roberta contributes to the $16 billion women spend each year on beauty products, but not because she has been sold on them by the $1.5 billion spent on cosmetic and toiletry advertising. She is using these fixes to try to present herself each day as a willing worker with her private life completely under her control.

Makeup and hairdos, however, are not enough to change the facts of life that show up on our face and body. More and more women (and men) are turning to plastic surgery; the surgeon takes away skin that has sagged and fat that has bagged. The nose gets a youthful slant up, the chin appears firmer, the eyes are more rested-looking, the wrinkles less deep. This type of fix can be expensive and often involves serious surgical procedures. My biggest concern is that we are too often not realistic about what is being fixed. If we want to fix eyelids that are drooping enough to make our eyes feel tired or look tired, surgery can fix the problem. If we want to fix our feeling that life has passed us by, that our time was misspent, that our husband was not faithful, that our children are grown, that our job has joined the new technologies and we haven't, or that we waited too long to begin a family, the plastic surgery will not be a fix.

But if makeovers and face fixes are for our own delight rather than our desperation, the meaning of the fix is quite different. Furthermore, the better we look to ourselves, the better we seem to *feel*. Have you ever caught sight of yourself in a mirror and thought, "My goodness, I look sick"? And then *felt* sick or monitored your aches and pains until you were convinced that you were indeed sick? Or, on the other hand, sat in a restaurant with smoky pink mirrors and saw your reflection as really radiant? Then enjoyed a meal letting your seductive and dramatic side match your image? I certainly have, and so have the women I've interviewed. The moral? Appearance can be a powerful placebo. The real seductiveness, drama, and verve come from inside. Don't wait for the right lighting and lipstick to let it out.

Are there real fixes for these feelings? Accepting that what has passed has passed, whether it be years or tears or both, is the beginning. Next is to decide how you want to live from here on. No do-overs of the past, but many real-life makeovers for the future. Decide how you want to organize or reorganize your family, your work time, and your play time. Take over decisions about your life as much as you can. And don't leave out your appearance. Exercise for beauty as well as health. Eat for beauty as well as health. And certainly enjoy your makeovers—as a small comfort but great fun!

Fixing Life Traumas

Traumas, the life crises that can make women reach for a new fix or start up an old one, can take many forms. They are types of intrusions, threats, injuries, attacks, impediments, and disappointments. What they have in common is that they all feel beyond our immediate control.

INTRUSIONS This group includes the obscene phone call that comes in the middle of the night, the robbery we find has been committed while we were at work, or the uninvited sexual advance.

THREATS Women experience lovers' infidelities, drunken drivers, and bosses' ultimatums as threats to their security and control.

INJURIES Sometimes the injuries are to our bodies, but sometimes our self-image is damaged. Either requires readjustment and a period of recuperation during which we are vulnerable to quick fixes.

ATTACKS Most women experience attacks on their children as even more traumatic than attacks on themselves. Any attack reduces our feelings of being comfortable in the world. At that point, we might reach for the wrong fortification.

IMPEDIMENTS When our goals are blocked, we all experience frustration. For women this may mean sexism interfering with a career choice, an ex-husband who limits her mobility, or a school system that will not deal with her exceptional child.

DISAPPOINTMENTS Disappointments are not exclusive to women. Disappointments in love, work, and friendships are part of life. But a woman is expected to carry on in all her other roles when she has experienced a disappointment in one. To do this, she too often props herself up or quiets herself down with quick fixes and small comforts.

Traumas are not always unexpected. They can be life events that wear and tear on us until we no longer even know which fix to reach for. For five years, I asked audiences of women to hand in their own version of a life events scale, similar to the one you may have seen developed by Thomas Holmes and Richard Rahe in 1967 called the Social Readjustment Rating Scale. That list starts with death of a spouse as the most traumatic and ends with minor violations of the law (like finding a parking ticket on your windshield) as the least traumatic but still worth counting.

Since the scale was developed for both men and women, the stress value placed on many traumas did not take into account how often the event had greater impact on women than on men, nor how many more events would be included on a Women's Life Events Scale.

Compare the two scales below. On the left is the Holmes and Rahe Scale and the "readjustment" point value for each. These points were the results of an averaging of all the assessments by women and men in their sample. On the right is my Women's Life Events Scale, revised by more than 2,000 women across the country who have come to my lectures on Women's Wellness. Notice how different are the point values and how many more traumas are added.

SOCIAL READJUSTMENT RATING SCALE *(abbreviated)*		WOMEN'S LIFE EVENTS SCALE	
Event	Points	Event	Points
Death of spouse	100	Death of spouse	100
Divorce	73	Divorce	100!
***		Illness of child, parent,	
Marital separation	65	spouse	100!
Death of close family		Marital separation	90!
member	63	Death of close family	
Personal illness or injury	53	member	80!
Marriage	50	Personal illness or injury	50
***		Marriage	100!
Fired at work	47	Remarriage	100!
Marital reconciliation	45	Fired at work	50
Retirement	45	Marital reconciliation	50
***		Retirement	50
Pregnancy	40	Husband's retirement	100!
***		Pregnancy	80!
***		Miscarriage/infertility	100!
Sex difficulties	39	Menopause	50!
Death of a close friend	37	Sex difficulties	80!
Son or daughter leaving		Death of a close friend	70!
home	29	Son or daughter leaving	
***		home	50
		Son or daughter returning	
		home	50!
		Trouble with in-laws	80!
Trouble with in-laws	29	Change in residence	70!
Change in residence	20	Planning a wedding	50!
***		Not planning a wedding	
***		(groom's mother)	50!
Vacation	13	Vacation	30!
Christmas	12	Christmas	50!

(The complete Holmes and Rahe Scale is reprinted in Appendix C. Items which were the same in score and content on the Women's Life Events Scale were omitted here. None of the Holmes and Rahe items were dropped by the new scale.)

It's fascinating to compare the items and scores that an all-female group would list compared to a mixed and averaged group. For women, for example, Christmas means buying, cooking, wrapping, exchanging, and cleaning, and all on no extra time. For women, vacations mean packing, unpacking, arrangements for the children and pets—and we blame our upset stomachs on the water! For women, relocation means that we meet the new butcher, baker, gasoline attendant, and PTA president. For women, divorce means we don't divorce the children and we do need more income. And the death of a friend or the illness of our child? How in the world can we fix that? In reality, there are no quick fixes for most life traumas. Rather, realistic preparation, perspective, and recuperation are the long-term remedies.

Fixing a Fast Pace Profile

Though it would be convenient to blame our addictions, dependencies, and fast fixes on our reactions to life's traumas, changes, and child-rearing mixed messages, we must examine the ways in which we may be setting ourselves up for fast fixes. The Fast Pace Profile you took in the previous chapter is the starting point for self-examination. Did you find that you tend to be a stimulus junkie, a phone phobic, and a perfectionist? Sometimes? Usually? If you hate to wait, as all Type A men and Fast Pace women do, then you will surely look for quick fixes to quiet your impatience and frustration.

Freedom from the need for fast fixes is often a gift. It can be given to you by parents when you are young. Parents who give a child unconditional acceptance of her shortcomings as well as her virtues, and love that is not contingent on perfect performance, teach her that she does not need to "fix" herself. In *Treating Type A Behavior and Your Heart*, Dr. Meyer

Friedman and Diane Ulmer suggest that it is particularly important for a girl to feel "special" in her father's eyes as well as her mother's. Fathers who have the patience to notice their daughters' small victories teach them patience and self-worth. I find that mothers who do the same, not only with their daughters but with themselves, set up the best role models of all.

If this type of acceptance was not a present from your family, today is the day to begin to parent yourself. You might not become fix-free overnight, but don't think you can't change yourself. Here is how to begin:

- Develop knowledge of what you *can* do rather than lists of what you should do.
- Practice delegating responsibility, and then *don't check* until the job is done. Whether at home or at the office, just because you can do it better doesn't mean that you should do it at all! Give others a chance to develop a sense of competency—with your approval and blessing.
- If you catch yourself dwelling on future fantasies or past glories, bring yourself into the present. Look carefully around to see what is chasing you away from living in the here-and-now. Then do something about the problem! Take control, rather than taking off.
- Remind yourself that it is fine to laugh out loud and to show affection openly. Both will give you laughter and affection in return—and these are real fixes which really do help us get through any day.
- Don't confuse disappointments with failures. Disappointments are realistic reactions when things don't work out the way you would want them to. Failures are our disappointments seen the way we think others see us. Since we can't read minds, let's not even try.

50

Every time you are hazy about why you are reaching for fixes, reread this chapter. Every time you feel alone with your addiction, compulsion, or dependency, reread the cases and interviews throughout the book. Every time you need a reminder that you can fix your fixes, reread the last chapter, Real Fixes. But remember, if you are fast-paced, knee-deep in traumas, and wrestling with difficult feelings, change takes time.

Take the first step toward change by honestly confronting the dependencies and addictions that are your fast fixes, big fixes, small comforts, or even fixes that kill. Then take the next step and give yourself the time and patience and attention and love you give to others. Use this time and attention to identify what needs fixing in your life, and then begin to sort and solve your problems with all the resources you have and all the help the pages to follow offer.

THREE

Food Fixes: To Eat or Not to Eat

Females and food have a very complicated relationship. We are the source of milk for our infants, the nutritionist for our children, and the dinner partner for our mate. We are in charge of family feasts and holiday treats. We outnumber men as supermarket shoppers by almost 90 percent. Yet 60 percent of women are trying not to eat at this very moment! In fact, 25 percent of women in the United States diet all their lives!

"I just look at food and I gain weight. Or maybe it's all the testing I do when I cook."

"I gained about thirty pounds with each baby and lost twenty—I have three kids so that's quite a lot of extra poundage to be lugging around. About once a year I decide, 'It's time,' but I never get rid of much of it. Oh well, I told my husband that when he gets rid of his belly, I'll get rid of mine."

"I'm always on a diet. I also hate to throw away food, so when I get the dinner plates into the kitchen I always eat the leftover mashed potatoes and half piece of pie someone left on their plate. I guess that's why I'm always on a diet."

"Food shopping is about the only legitimate shopping we can afford, so it's my only opportunity to sneak in some luxuries for myself—cupcakes, fancy cookies, or tarts from the bakery."

Most of us gain about 20 pounds while we are feeding our family for three decades. Most of us say that we would want 15 pounds to disappear for us to be happy with our weight. Yet most of us cannot stop eating! Among the hundreds and hundreds of women who contributed to my research for this book, food figured in every category of fixes. For some, food is a fast fix; for some, it is a secret fix; and for some, it is a fix that literally or figuratively kills!

The Fastest Favorite Fix

When most women want to make themselves feel better, food is their fastest focus. It's available, instantly gratifying, and leaves no immediate evidence. Food may not be most women's only fix. For example, reaching for alcohol, too, is most characteristic of women who are single or young married. Widows tell me they also throw themselves into housework, sewing, and reorganizing closets. Teenage women sleep their problems off. But all women, in all age groups, whether married, single, divorced, or widowed, told me they eat as their quickest fix! Of the more than 1,000 women who filled out Quick Fix survey forms, the following percentage in each age group and marital status group said they found food as their most constant quick fix.

What do they eat? It depends on what needs fixing. Chocolate seems to be the number-one fix of all. If Dr. Michael Liebowitz of the New York State Psychiatric Institute is correct,

Percent	Age	Marital Status
55	20–29	Married
65	30–39	Married
55	40–49	Married
75	over 50	Married
70	20–60+ (½ in 20s)	Single
50	20–60+	Divorced
55	40–60+	Widowed

one reason is that many women are probably *phenylethylamine-*sensitive. Phenylethylamine is an amphetaminelike chemical, which, Dr. Liebowitz suggests, is produced by the brain when we are infatuated. Like other stimulants, it boosts our energy, cuts our appetite, and makes us believe that the future is ours. Chocolate contains phenylethylamine. Any wonder that some of us crave chocolate when we break up a romance? Any wonder why we can cuddle up to a box of chocolate in bed? Any wonder why men give women chocolate on Valentine's Day?

Even if research demonstrates that phenylethylamine is not sufficiently absorbed into the system by eating chocolate, women will tell you that chocolate still provides the high Dr. Liebowitz describes. The cocoa in chocolate is also a stimulant; the sugar is energizing; the candy is rich and filling. These are not "empty" calories! And the associations are seductive. Hot cocoa from Mommy when we were cold, chocolate in the candy dish when company visited, boxes of chocolate and bunches of roses from an admirer, chocolate kisses, chocolate bunnies, chocolate cake . . . When we feel we need to *sweeten our lives* or *fill ourselves with love*, chocolate seems to be the favorite fix.

In my survey, other sweets and ice cream came next as the foods women abuse most. They are ever-present at birthday parties, PTA receptions, Girl Scout meetings, after-school snacks, office galas, dinner parties, or trips through town with our children. Many women crave sugars and carbohydrates premenstrually and forget to stop craving them when PMS passes. Like chocolate, these foods symbolically sweeten up our life. They are what we use to reward ourselves after we've been through a hard day. They remind us of childhood parties and more carefree times. And they give us a rush of blood sugar, short-lived though it might be.

Junk food and fast foods come next as quick fixes. We stock junk foods as snacks for our children, as fillers for an instant meal, as emergency rations for unexpected company—and then we eat them when we need a fast treat. Fast foods have certainly earned their name. They are not only available quickly, but they are consumed quickly. We don't even need plates and forks.

Lynne was feeling very guilty. She had stopped at a drive-through chicken restaurant and picked up six "pieces" for dinner. She had been feeling particularly tired all day and didn't have the strength to resist the aroma of the chicken. She opened the easy-open box at the next traffic light and wrapped a drumstick in a napkin. Two lights later, she finished off a second piece. After a few fries, she felt tired and full—and guilty. What was she going to say about the small order when she got home? She decided to say that she hadn't bought any for herself because she wasn't hungry. As everyone else was eating, she made herself a sandwich so she could join her family.

Pasta and breads are ever-popular as quick fixes since they remind us of home-cooked meals. That is, meals cooked in somebody else's home. Usually our childhood home. Our grandmother's home. Our favorite friend's home. Any home but the one in which we have to do the cooking! They are very filling foods and give us the feeling that we have stocked up on nutrition. Although both are indeed nutritious in small amounts combined with proteins, vegetables, and fruits, we tend to eat these foods as fixes, not as nutrition. A big bowl of pasta is more than we need. Half a loaf of delicious, warm bread with butter and jelly or cheese goes far beyond our nutritional requirements —but often not beyond our emotional requirements. Have you surprised yourself when you have realized how much you've just eaten while you were reading or chatting on the phone? I have!

Feeding Ourselves

Like shopping, food can be used as our fast track to feeling filled when we are empty, fortified when we feel weak physically or psychologically, rewarded when we feel unappreciated, energized when we feel tired, cared for when we feel homesick, and childlike when we feel old. We know that the remedy is very temporary, but if it's the only one we allow ourselves, it is the one we will reach for. If it is the only one we think we deserve, the real problems will not be addressed or remedied. The fast fixes will soon be needed again. In our effort to stay independent, we will become food-dependent. In our effort to keep going, we will have to stop again and again for our food fix.

Food as a Secret Fix

The secret food fix or secret snack becomes a problem only when it is motivated by an anxiety rather than an appetite. Remember, female fast fixes are usually attempts at making daily life better, not worse. If a snack is a mid-afternoon apple that relieves hunger and keeps you going until dinner, you really *have* fixed a minor crisis quickly and efficiently. But if you are biting into an apple because you really want to bite off your boss's head, the fix won't work. After you have finished the apple, the urge to bite will still be pushing at you. Next you may try to bite into some oatmeal cookies, then peanut brittle, and then some hard candy. True, you may have "fixed" your urge to be aggressive, but you will probably have gained 10 pounds by the end of the month and the problems with your boss will be still unfixed. The bigger problem that needed fixing—finding an appropriate way of handling your anxiety about your anger —also remains.

Fast food is so available to women as a fast fix that it is not surprising so many women have trouble controlling their eating. We talk about different types of eating problems throughout this book. In this instance, the secret snacks to which I refer are not signs of compulsive eating or *bulimia*. Secret snacks are meant to satisfy a hunger within—and don't. They are snacks that make us feel as if we just consumed 300 calories and forgot to enjoy them. Or put food into our mouths and no longer remember what we ate. Or grabbed for something sweet when our lives needed sweetening, not our mouths. Or snacked out of boredom, or busyness, or frustration, or habit.

It is no wonder we want to keep these snacks secret. They are usually meant to help us keep our mouths busy and closed. Why would we then open our mouths to tell the world about our snacks?

Snacking Pattern Profile

If you would like to understand your snacking patterns, ask yourself the following questions:

1. Do you reach for home-style food when you'd like to be back home as a kid again, rather than running your own home?

2. Do you reach for chocolate when your emotional life needs a boost?

3. Do you reach for crunchy food when you want to chew someone out?

4. Do you reach for elaborate snack combos when you are bored?

5. Do you reach for soft, mushy pastries when you feel like babying yourself?

6. Do you reach for exotic delights when you'd really like to get out of your everyday life and into a vacation?

7. Do you reach for the foods you were not allowed to have as a child when you're feeling particularly defiant as an adult?

8. Do you reach for big sandwiches when you have a hefty project?

9. Do you reach for the cake recipe and ingredients when you'd rather not reach for the overdue paperwork?

10. Do you reach for anything to eat, just to have an excuse to stop and sit for a moment?

Do your answers to these questions give you a picture of your snacking patterns? Most women say "yes" to most of these questions and can add a few questions of their own. Your answers are telling you that the real secret may not be the snack you are hiding from others, but the reason for the snacking, which you are hiding from yourself.

The textbook term for this kind of behavior is *displacement*. You are redirecting impulses that may frighten or upset you and the people around you toward less upsetting outlets. You find that you fix your wanderlust by drinking a piña colada instead of running away from home. Fix your procrastination by constructive baking instead of destructive self-blame. Fix your fatigue by time out for a snack rather than time off on strike. Fix your dependency fantasies by eating Mama's pasta instead of running back to Mama's home. Fix your anger by biting a breadstick rather than making biting comments.

Actually, displacement sounds like a practical problem solver so far. Often it is not. Displacement may save your happy home or job from your displeasures and dangerous demonstrations, but it does not change your displeasures or disappointments. If those impulses and needs keep pushing at you, snacking will soon not do the trick. Guilt about your unacceptable impulses will seep into your day. Soon you will be snacking more, enjoying it less, and feeling more and more guilty. Snacking more as you displace more. Enjoying less as the real problem grows. Feeling guilty about the original impulse *plus* the snacking solution. The original problem has now been multiplied threefold.

Why We Secretly Snack

If secret snacking is a fast fix for you that is backfiring, your first step is to stop for a moment before you reach for a snack and ask yourself if your snack-to-be is a *distraction*, an *avoidance trick*, or a *substitution*.

If your snack is distraction, concentrate fully on the thought or feeling you have been trying to put out of your mind. Are you feeling stranded because the car battery is dead? Are you feeling annoyed because your guests tonight are boring clients? Are you worried because you have a yearly checkup tomorrow? Then ask yourself if a snack makes sense as a fix. Your answer will usually be "no." Food will not make the car run, your guests go away, or your checkup less worrisome. Ask yourself what might be a more constructive activity than snacking—perhaps a call to car-rental agencies, a plan for an after-dinner walk with your guests, or ten minutes of music while you are stretched out on the sofa.

If your snack is an avoidance trick, admit it to yourself. Ask yourself how long the snack will permit you to procrastinate. Long enough to make the calories worthwhile? Probably not. It is more practical either to make that call or do that chore and finish with enough time to relax afterward, or to make a conscious decision to put off the activity and take the consequences.

If your snack is a substitution for something you don't feel you should or could want, reexamine your assumptions. Maybe you are not getting what you want because you are not asking for it: more help with the house, more fun on the weekends, or more love from your loved ones. Maybe you are not getting what you want because you haven't admitted to yourself that you have certain needs and wants: more time for yourself, more achievement for yourself, or more recognition for yourself. Maybe, maybe, maybe. The important point is to try to fix the real problem with a real solution, not a substitution. You have nothing to lose but calories by trying.

If you find that your eating doesn't fall into these categories and that your snack is an appropriate response to a hint of hunger, go ahead and enjoy it. Then tell someone how good it was so that you can practice not feeling guilty! But if your answer to any or all of the questions was "yes," sit down for a minute before you snack.

Safe Snacking Tips

After examining your secret snacking for hidden hungers, you may find that the snacking habit still keeps you reaching for food when you'd prefer to pass. If the habit is hard to break, try these tips from women around the country.

1. Schedule your snacks. Allow yourself in-between mini-meals, but plan them as you would your three big meals. Decide what you will eat and when. This way, snacks won't snowball into constant eating, nor will they be so secret that you forget to enjoy them.
2. Domesticate your snacks. Dilute them. Housebreak them. Instead of straight cola, mix it with club soda. Instead of straight ice cream, top off fresh fruit with a small scoop. Make an open sandwich—one piece of bread. Don't deprive yourself of a snack, but certainly control its consequences. Lower sugars, calories, and cholesterol so that the quick fix doesn't hurt you in the long run.
3. Institutionalize your snacks. Add rituals to them. Set up a small table near the window for your afternoon or mid-morning bite. Bring a placemat to the office for your coffee break. Like British teatime, invite a friend to join you at your desk or snack spot for a spot of relaxation.

Compulsive Eating

Compulsive eating is the continued use of food to fix all problems. Why would women reach for food fixes despite guilt or shame? Some of the reasons women have given me are:

TO AVOID FAILURE Eating can be a way to avoid doing something at which you can fail, such as taking on a new responsibility at work or at home, taking a take-home exam, or writing a difficult letter. Examples: A sandwich before studying an elusive subject, fussing with dinner for your dinner party until it's too late to fix your own appearance, or grabbing enough breakfast to make you late for your driving test.

TO ALLEVIATE ANXIETY New situations bring on anxiety. Reporting to a new job, moving to a new neighborhood, or going to a party where you don't know anyone are a few examples. Many women say these situations kick up an unhealthy appetite for snacking days and days in advance of the anxiety situation.

FOR REVENGE Compulsive eating can be a way to get back at someone with whom you're angry. Gaining weight may be a way of silently saying, "See what you are doing to me? You are starving me emotionally and I am eating to fix my feeling of emptiness." Or a way of saying, "I'll get even with you for loving me for who I am outside instead of inside by getting fat!" The compulsive eater usually has a convenient scapegoat to blame and often avoids blaming herself.

TO AVOID INTIMACY A woman who is having love problems sometimes finds it easier to avoid the confrontations and pain. Food gives her a substitute for other pleasures, and real or imaginary obesity gives her an excuse to avoid men. If you spend a lot of time binging, there's no room left for intimacy— not even a desire for it. It's a vicious circle, since binging can also be a quick fix for the emptiness and emotional void created when love problems cause a poor sexual relationship.

The Diet Dilemma

Does a diet really fix anything besides our thighs—temporarily? Of course it does—temporarily.

- A diet gives us a goal.
- A diet gives us a feeling of control over at least a part of our life—eating.

o A diet gives us a chance to focus on ourselves—too
   often the very person we neglect.

But the operative word in dieting is "temporarily." A real
goal, sense of control, and self-improvement plan must focus
on a change in eating habits, not a crash diet. More fruits and
fresh vegetables, and less ice cream and candy, should be permanent revisions in your eating routine. Anything less than a
total change in food philosophy and the weight is back in no
time.

We all know that more than half of us go on and off diets
regularly. Some of us like diets that require that we measure our
food portions. Some of us weigh our food. Some of us follow
doctors' diets, some follow fad diets, some concoct our own
diets. Some join groups and some keep our diets secret. But
most of us have dieted sometime if not most of the time.

A diet is a fix in every sense of the word. It is a way to fix
our body. It is a way to fix our fear of aging. It is something we
can give ourselves when we need more attention. It is a food fix.
As much as a diet tells us what not to eat, it also tells us what
we can eat. Every food on the list becomes a fix. In a sense, a
diet is a fix in the way that an addiction is a fix. We experience
discomfort on withdrawal: fear of gaining, fear of loss of control
over our eating, fear of loss of health.

Even if we didn't see diets as fixes, the media would soon
convince us that a diet could fix almost anything. Here are
actual headlines from women's magazines over the last three
years:

FROM JIGGLES AND FLAB TO TONED AND SEXY IN JUST
   12 WEEKS

THE EAT-ALL-DAY DIET

SHEDDING 25 INCHES AND 25 POUNDS

QUICK DIETS YOU CAN TRUST

HOW NOT TO BE FAT AFTER THIRTY-FIVE

THOSE LAST 5 POUNDS—DON'T LOSE THEM, USE
  THEM

30 MINUTES TO THIN

HELP STAMP OUT CELLULITE!

HOW THE SUN CAN HELP YOU DIET

An editor of a national women's magazine confided that
every cover of her magazine features at least one diet article
each issue. This confirmed my suspicions that we are learning
how to diet more often than how to eat right.

Although one third of us do need to lose weight for health
reasons, at least 60 percent of American women fall within the
National Institutes of Health weight guidelines. Why, then, do
we diet anyway?

Some of the women I interviewed explain:

"I think thinner bodies look younger, but not when
stretched skin hangs. So I diet now to look younger later."

"I start a diet each new season when I see the clothes cata-
logues filled with clothes that would make me look ridiculous. After I lose some weight, I buy these clothes, then
gain the weight back and get angry at myself."

"I really think that women are more worried about getting
undressed before bed than men are worried about performing in bed! So I diet to feel sexier and less inhibited."

"I know genetics gave me thighs, but I can't help thinking that they are my fault, not my inheritance. So I diet and diet, and work out, and diet."

"I diet just-in-case. Just in case I have to fly to Acapulco to lie in the sun. Just in case I have a new lover. Dieting is my form of fantasizing, I guess."

"I do a diet do-over at least once a year. It makes me very self-righteous. I guess it's my competitiveness coming out. I feel better than everyone who is stuffing their face. I feel like I am ahead of them in the thinness race."

The majority of women I interviewed told me that their most serious dieting coincided with serious life changes. They dieted before their wedding, after their divorce, or when their marriage was in trouble. Many worried when they noticed their husbands were dieting because they feared the men were "getting in shape to run."

Again and again we can see how women have been taught to value appearances. Looking good is confused with feeling good. We have talked about how we are also taught to stay in control. Being in control of our food might then be equated with being in control of our life or fears or events. We see others dieting and feel that they are getting ahead of us, or leaving us behind—literally.

The reality is that dieting can only fix an overweight problem. It does not change our life, our control over the man in our world, or our control over our aging. Stay thin if it makes you feel better about yourself. Not for anyone else. And not too thin. The latest reports are that being too thin is as unhealthy as being too fat. Didn't you suspect that all along?

Another reality is that after eighteen years of age, the weight that you put on will no longer be evenly distributed throughout your body. By twenty-five, you will be able to see your figure's future! It's while in their twenties that for the first time many of my patients complain that they can begin to see similarities between their changing shape and their mother's shape. By thirty-five, estrogen will encourage your weight to gather on your belly, thighs, and hips. Dieting alone is not enough to dent your destiny, but exercise and toning and planned menus will work. Just as dieting alone will not change your contours, exercising alone will only add muscle bulk under your fat. If you really want a figure fix, consult your doctor and start on an eating and exercise plan for life.

Food as a Fatal Fix

What does food mean to you? Whether or not what you eat should be decided by your need for nutrition, your need to keep yourself and the people you love going strong. If your attitude about food is healthy, you see the dinner table as an opportunity for togetherness.

Your attitude about eating is less healthy if food has turned into a coping mechanism for you: a substitute for love, a symbol for control, or a stress soother. It is less than healthy thinking about food, preparing it, eating it, or avoiding it take up too much time in your life! Food can be a fast fix or a secret fix. It can also be a fatal fix. Bulimia, binging in a short period of time (a few hours), is an example. In the case that follows, bulimia became *bulimarexia*, in which the binger rids herself of the food.

Laurie's home life had been abnormal for as long as she could remember. Her mother, an extremely slim, attractive woman and successful decorating consultant, was also an alcoholic who relied on Laurie to help her off the floor every night, clean her up, and roll her into bed. Laurie's father, disgusted by his wife's behavior, often refused to speak with her except through Laurie.

"Looking back on it, I can see that there were two pressures in the house that led me to binge eating," says Laurie. "One, my mother put a lot of emphasis on appearance. And two, nobody really seemed to nurture me. I was kind of forgotten in the mess."

Throughout her teens and twenties, Laurie looked forward to any occasion where food would be served. "I would eat tremendous amounts of food," she says. "It was disgusting. Then I would go throw up. Sometimes it would be once or twice a day, or sometimes I would go for a month without doing it. But I could never really get rid of the idea."

By the time she was thirty, Laurie had experienced many of the side effects of her condition, bulimarexia: a sore throat, sore stomach muscles, loss of tooth enamel due to gastric acid, fatigue, constipation, weakness, and depression. Laurie knows that other risks of bulimia are irregular heartbeat and sudden death. She has been in therapy with a special eating-disorders psychologist for several years now and is still struggling to get control of her eating.

Anorexia nervosa, the intense fear of becoming obese that doesn't go away even after a dramatic loss of weight, can also be fatal. Carter's college roommate tells the story:

All we knew was that Carter was getting thinner and thinner, and that she was spending more and more time over at the gym. She constantly boasted about how strong she was, and in fact she had developed a wiry strength that astonished us. But she never boasted about her lovely, willowy body. Standing in front of the mirror, she would poke at some nonexistent flab and say, "Look at this! I can't *stand* how fat I am." I mean, we could see her ribs. At mealtimes, Carter would take a little salad and some soup, and stop eating after a few mouthfuls. "It's a *tremendous* amount of food," she would say, as if it were obvious to all of us.

We were so naive then. Carter was pre-med, so we figured she knew what she was doing. It's a good thing her advisor was the kind of woman who wasn't afraid to get involved. She called Carter's parents and took us all into a little group and gave Carter's symptoms a name: anorexia nervosa. She told us that some girls who are conflicted about sex or stressed about academic performance occasionally react like Carter did.

Carter's parents came to school and got her. At Christmas break I went to see her in the hospital. She had lost about 30 pounds and weighed about 89. Since she still wouldn't eat enough to keep herself alive, they were feeding her through an intravenous tube. She never came back to college.

What on earth would cause a woman to eat, or not eat, to the point that it threatens her life? A classic interpretation of Carter's disorder would be as follows: Pressures applied by her mother and father to be a "good girl" sexually and to work hard toward being a doctor pushed her, subconsciously, into a solution that actually worked for her. By starving her body, she removed the breasts and hips that might attract men. As for academic demands, she was now free of any pressure to become a doctor—she was too sick. Perhaps no one had asked her if medicine was her own passion. Food was the only thing in her life she could control. She "fixed up" her life the dangerous way.

Researchers who have studied bulimia and anorexia have not yet come up with universal answers. Hormones may be the connection between craving or starving behaviors for some women, but social and emotional factors better explain other cases. And what of the bulimarexic? She binges and then phobically gets rid of the food by vomiting, taking laxatives, overexercising, or using diuretics. She looks like an anorexic but acts like a bulimic.

In all three cases (anorexia, bulimia, and bulimarexia), most victims of these attempts to fix feelings with food manipulations are women. The reason these disorders are predominantly female problems may be because stress predisposes us to eating disturbances in general, and society patterns our behaviors in particular. We live in a society that offers too much food but tells women not to eat it. We all know the "ideal" body weight by looking at the emaciated models in the magazines and the boyish bodies in movies. Lately, women have begun to question this ideal. Even the height/weight body charts have been adjusted upwards by insurance companies and medical facilities.

Most of us have been compulsive about eating at some point in our lives, but we have not really been anorectic, bulimic, or bulimarexic. If you are, seek professional care! This book is just your starting point. Medical treatment, psychotherapy, family counseling, and group support is usually necessary. Save your life!

Diagnosing Eating Disorders

Step number one in solving an eating disorder is recognizing it. If you're not sure you have an eating disorder, ask yourself these questions:

1. **"Am I behaving in a consistent pattern?"** For example, do you binge regularly, purge regularly? Do you exercise regularly—far longer and more regularly than you used

to and to the point where people comment that it's not healthy?

2. **"Is the behavior interfering with my life?"** Although eating or not eating were originally supposed to make your life better, once they get out of hand you can be very busy trying to keep your life running smoothly. Are you spending more time in the doctor's office than usual? Do you leave work undone at the office so you can rush home to begin your binge? Are you spending so much money on food that it has affected the cash flow in your household?

3. **"Do people tell me I'm going too far? That I have no time for friends and family?"** Do you prefer sitting in front of the television with your binge food to visiting with friends? Do you avoid parties because you know you won't be able to control your eating behavior? Do you prefer eating alone to eating with others because it is so hard to find a way to get away from the table to purge?

4. **"Am I putting unrealistic standards of slimness on myself?"** Do you ignore *your* bone structure when you conjure up your ideal image?

Getting Help

You can be sure that there is care available for the bulimic, anorectic, bulimarexic, or compulsive overeater who wants care. If you have an eating disorder and are ready for help, try a hospital or ask for a referral from your own doctor. You don't even have to do it in person—you can call up and not identify yourself. Psychiatrists and psychologists can often help or refer. Overeaters Anonymous has helped many women. Dentists often detect bulimia because of the dental damage and may have a source of help at hand in their Rolodex.

Although anorexia, bulimia, bulimarexia, and compulsive overeating are different conditions, some of the advice for treating them applies to all three:

o **Read.** There are a number of good books available. Dr. Richard Ganley, a senior psychologist at the Renfrew Center in Philadelphia, suggests *Feeding the Hungry Heart* by Geneen Roth (Bobbs, 1982). For information on family dynamics, in other words what happens inside the family structure to predispose someone toward an eating disorder, he recommends *The Golden Cage: The Enigma of Anorexia Nervosa* by Hilde Bruch (Harvard University Press, 1978).

o **Talk to friends, family, and appropriate colleagues**—not necessarily about every last detail of your eating habit but rather about the factors that are precipitating it. Is your job unduly stressful? Speak to the boss. Are your parents setting your goals for you? Sit down with them and clarify their role in your life as you see it—or simply smile at their advice, thank them for it, and quietly set your own goals. Is your husband insistent that you be slim? Tell him that you expect him to tighten up his belly and get a hair transplant, and see how he takes it.

o **Base your decisions to change on your own desire,** not on a desire to please someone else. It's important to recognize that *you* are the most important person in this healing process.

o **Don't expect your recovery to be immediate** or without an occasional step backward.

o **Keep busy!** Join a health club, take a course, do volunteer work, take up horseback riding . . . do *anything* to shift your attention away from yourself and out into the big, busy world.

o **Think positive thoughts about yourself.** You can overcome your disorder. Won't it be great when you no longer feel the lure of your fast fix? Your behavior is under your own control. Your food addiction is not a biochemical addiction like a narcotic addiction, thank goodness. So you can begin to detox today!

For bulimics, bulimarexics, and all overeaters:

o **Avoid being alone when you are most susceptible.** Don't let yourself be isolated if you know that food will be your company. Plan ahead!

o **Focus on immediate rewards and past successes.** Overeaters can think not about how much better life will be years from now, but how much better you'd feel today if you could get past a twenty-four-hour period without binging. Think about other immediate rewards: not having to feel guilty, or still having the money you would have spent on food.

o **Don't be inactive!** Inactivity is a double problem. It provides more eating time and less appetite reduction. Exercise, dancing, even brisk walking or closet cleaning usually cut our appetite for a while and burn up calories as a bonus. If your new activity takes you out of the house, you may also meet new people and begin to round out your needs in social ways instead of weight-gaining ways. Form a babysitting cooperative or a food-shopping consortium if your needs are more practical than social. You'll get both social and practical support that way—and will have less time and need for food as a fix.

For everyone:

o **Fight perfectionism!** The world, as I'm sure you have noticed, is not perfect. Not one person you know is perfect. Why should you try to be perfect? You probably don't love your child or parent or friends or spouse any less for their lack of perfection. Perhaps their shortcomings help you feel useful and needed. Don't love yourself any less for your lack of perfection. Don't set unrealistic standards for yourself that will lead you to be pessimistic about your ability to be loved or enjoyed. Pessimism creates self-fulfilling prophecies of gloom and doom. Of course you'll never start to get control over eating if you have a big bone structure and set Cher up as your standard for beauty. Why bother, you'll say. Don't find excuses, I say. Set up a realistic goal for your own body and health, and then take control.

FOUR

Shopping Fixes: When the Going Gets Tough, the Tough Go Shopping

Is it true that inside every women is a compulsive shopper longing to be let loose in a downtown department store?

Is it true that a woman cannot refuse a bargain—whether she needs it or not?

Is it true that women get as "high" on shopping as men get on gambling, fighting, or racing?

Is it true that women prefer shopping to sex?

If we were to believe the jokes about women and shopping, told by men, of course, we would say "true" to all of the above. My interviews with men lead me to suspect that they may want to believe that women are interested in shopping above everything else. Why? Maybe because providing women with money could well be the only way many men know how to give. If they believe we would prefer to be bought off, how much less anxiety they must feel about giving affection or making love.

Buying to Keep Busy

In truth, my interviews with women have taught me that most women shop to fill free moments in their busy day, or empty spaces in their crowded emotional lives. Those who are filling in free moments with shopping are usually women who must always be occupied. Rushing through stores, signing and sending, returning and exchanging, feel like useful activities, and leave little time to think thoughts that might be more unsettling than the shopping bill. Thoughts about biological clocks, about marital mismatches, about parents' aging, about choices or lack of choices, about illness past or illnesses that may come, about financial futures, about our sex lives, about our mixed feelings, confusions, and conflicts.

This type of shopping manages to avoid the problems that might come up if mixed feelings, confusions, and conflicts were allowed to surface to consciousness.

Donna is an account executive in an advertising agency. She also is a mother of two small children and the wife of a dentist. She gets up at six o'clock each morning to have breakfast with her children, and then commutes by car to her office. She describes her day as a continual crisis. She is the troubleshooter for the agency's clients and her own staff. She is also the troubleshooter for her husband and children. Calls from her husband's office and her children's school come in with almost as much frequency as calls from the interoffice intercom.

And what does Donna do on her lunch hour? She takes clients to lunch. Then what does she do? In the fifteen minutes between lunch and her next appointment back at the office, Donna shops. With reckless abandon she tests perfume for ten minutes, or buys stockings for eight minutes, or picks up a house gift for her mother-in-law for twenty-two minutes and runs back to the office late. And each time she asks herself, "Why didn't I just stroll back to the office and catch my breath before my afternoon appointments instead?"

Probably because Donna doesn't trust herself with any extra time. If she caught her breath, she might never want to lose it again. If she relaxed for a few minutes, she might get used to it. If she thought about her life, she might want to change it. Or, perhaps, she might have to admit that she doesn't want to change it. That she is not unhappy about being with adults all day instead of home with children. That she is not as much harried as happy to be so vital to her husband's daily life that he is unlikely ever to leave her. That being underpaid makes her feel less pressure to perform perfectly on the job. These are understandable thoughts and feelings, but perhaps not to Donna. The fix? To keep herself preoccupied with shopping.

Why wouldn't Donna blot out unsettling thoughts with drinking or drugs instead? This is not a simple question, but let's look at the information we have about Donna. She seems most comfortable when she is in control of her activities. She drives herself to work rather than letting a train carry her. She is willing to take the responsibility of being an account executive in exchange for the decision-making control it gives her. She would rather earn money than not have her own money. Shopping represents activity, decision making, and financial resources. Other fixes, like alcohol, tranquilizers, or affairs, represent a loss of control and power—a reliance on a chemical substance or another person. Shopping, in this case, is the fix that fits.

Trying to Buy What's Missing

Many women shop for a very different reason. Rather than using shopping to keep themselves too busy to let confusing or upsetting thoughts and feelings surface, they use shopping as a way of searching for something that's missing. Sometimes what is missing is companionship, sometimes it's self-pride, sometimes it's a sense of usefulness, sometimes what's missing is our own youth or our optimism about the future. Whatever it is that is missing, the sense of emptiness is the same. And so, too, is the remedy—shopping. We may buy clothes to cover ourselves, change our proportions, or state our style. We may buy perfume to announce our presence. We may buy jewelry to decorate our body. We may buy coats to keep ourselves warm. But after the shopping bags and the closets are full, the inner emptiness remains.

> "You're coming home with me," Pam would say to a sweater she fell in love with. "You're going to live in my closet now," she'd say to shoes as she looked at them in the store mirror. "I've got to have you" was her line for a piece of jewelry. She told me that a saleswoman overheard her one day and laughed. "You have more lines than a lonely bachelor at a singles bar," the saleswoman said to Pam.

What the saleswoman said made Pam think about her flirtation with "things." She wondered about her relationship with people. She knew she could choose "things," not people. She could give away "things," not people. She could return "things," not people. Although she knew "things" couldn't let her down, she admitted to herself that they could not bring her up more than temporarily. She began to wonder if people frightened her because they could not be bought and then packed away after the season. The more she thought, the less she bought. She began to look for a better fix for her emptiness.

Alone in the Fitting Room

Like Donna, many women use shopping to avoid having time to acknowledge thoughts and feelings that might unsettle their compromises and commitments. Like Pam, many women use shopping to fill feelings of emotional emptiness temporarily, mistaking purchase power for personal power. But the list of the ways in which shopping can be a quick fix does not end here! Listen to this letter:

> Shopping is the only private time I seem to have! It's just me, alone in the dressing room, trying on something for me alone. I usually don't buy anything unless I have a special occasion as an excuse, because we are short on money. But I picture myself at great places when I try on great clothes. It's like a mini-vacation for me when I go shopping. Then I go home to a very, very full household.

Obviously, for many, many of us, it's difficult to declare alone time without a good excuse. We think of ourselves as emergency-room doctors, police, air-traffic controllers, psychologists, nurses, chauffeurs, nutritionists, and efficiency experts all rolled into one—on call at least twenty-four hours a day. And we usually are! If the last good rest you gave yourself was when you stayed at the hospital after your baby was born, then you know what I mean. Shopping can be, for some, a way out of the house, where alone time is less obvious.

Don't Shout, Shop

For many women, shopping can be an outlet for anger. Here is how it can work:

> "I don't just shop. I go on a shopping rampage. I tear into clothes racks instead of my family. I buy with defiance when I don't need anything at all. I demand sales help when I feel neglected. I throw a fit when clothes don't fit. Then I

go home much calmer. I know it sounds adolescent, but I think it's my way of trying to control my temper at home. It's sometimes expensive, but it works for me."

Though shopping may lead to financial trouble in the long run, it starts so often as a short run to the nearest emotional relief. Men, we tell ourselves, are emotional children. They are expected to be grumpy or sulky. Children will be children, we tell ourselves. Their tantrums are expected. But *we* are supposed to be in control of our tempers. We are supposed to chart our premenstrual days so that we can control irritability. We are supposed to understand our in-laws' personalities so that we don't take their behavior personally. We are supposed to understand that repairmen run from two hours to two weeks late, so that we don't greet them with a grudge—or they'll never come again.

Since we are not supposed to be able to resist shopping, we often don't. Is it any wonder that there are far, far more women who are compulsive shoppers than men? Men are expected and allowed and even taught to be direct in their expression of frustration. Of course they are taught that it is better not to fight, but if they do find themselves in a fight, they are taught to win.

We are often taught how to lose gracefully. Men may call anger toward their sons constructive criticism; we are told we are harping. When fathers ground their daughters, they are being protective. What do our daughters say to us, their mothers? "You don't understand!" In the office, we are "just being a female" when we stiffen with affront. At least in the stores, we are doing what is expected of us. We have taken on shopping as a role assignment and use it for our own purposes.

The Spite Spree

Shopping is not always something we do for pleasure.

> "I was so angry at him for being stingy that I went shopping for all those extras that I never let myself buy—and charged them all to him. New makeup, two belts, a long cashmere scarf—you know. If he won't buy me presents, I'll buy me presents. And not from my salary, either. It's okay for me to buy his socks with my money, so I've decided it's okay for me to buy my treats with his money. And you know, when I got home, I didn't feel guilty, and I even felt better about him!"

Not all sour-grapes shopping sprees have such happy endings. Often the temporary relief from feeling deprived leads to weeks and months of arguments. Buying yourself gifts which you really want from others is a fix that fades fast! Your spree may have been an attempt to avoid admitting directly what you want or need from your partner, either to him or to yourself. You might have to admit that it's not gifts from a store you need but gifts of time, thoughtfulness, and love. If so, remember that it does count even if you have to ask for what you need.

Don't use that old excuse against your own best interest: "He should know what I want without my telling him." Tell him. If he doesn't hear you clearly, tell him again in a different way or with new language. And then when you buy yourself a gift, it can be from you to you—with love.

80

The Credit Card Crunch

"I shop and charge. I never pay cash or use a check. It wouldn't be the same. It would then make me feel like I was becoming poorer and poorer with each purchase. When I charge, my bank balance feels as if it stays the same. It's as if I can have it all—clothes, furniture, and a bank balance. Then the bills come in. I hate even opening the envelopes. Sometimes I don't because they make me too anxious. Many bills stay unpaid for too long. Help!"

Realistically, only household incomes greater than $30,000 can provide shopping money beyond the necessities. Yet 80 percent of American women have charge cards, and half charged more than $500 last year. Sounds low? The average charge for the year was almost $2,000! Obviously, some women just shop, but others buy. The letter above is from a woman who buys. She doesn't just browse, or bargain-hunt as a hobby, the way many women do. She buys. Buying on credit is, of course, even more expensive than paying on the spot because there are late charges and interest charges. There is also the value of the time that must be spent checking and writing and mailing the monthly bills. What can you do if this is you?

Get rid of your credit cards. Cut them up, give them to someone who can guard them for you until you have paid off your bills, someone who can throw them away for you, or make them useless by painting nail polish over the whole card. The main point is, if you know that you do not have control over your use of credit cards, don't own them. They will own you. They are a cash flow management tool, not a magical passport to shopping heaven. We laugh at ourselves when we talk about our problems with plastic, but we know that this fast fix can get us into a big fix.

Just-in-Case Consumers

"I am a 'just-in-case' shopper. I buy fabric and dress patterns and quilt designs just in case I ever have any extra time to work with my hands. I now have more than thirty-five boxes of material just in case I might have time to make a wall hanging. And if I use any of the fabric, I feel I must get some more to maintain a certain level."

"Just-in-case" shoppers are not restricted to quilters. There are "just-in-case" food shoppers, of course. Those of us who are ready for thirty of our acquaintances to drop in unexpectedly at any time for dinner. There are "just-in-case" gift shoppers. They pick up baby gifts, birthday gifts, housewarming gifts, anniversary gifts, Christmas gifts—just in case they don't have time at the time. There are "just-in-case" clothes shoppers, who buy formals although they have not been to one in years, jogging outfits although they do not exercise, and mini-skirts although they have not yet shed the necessary 15 pounds.

"Just-in-case" shoppers are usually compulsive shoppers. That is, although they are choosing items to buy, they do not have a choice about buying. Compulsive shoppers feel a tension build whenever they could be shopping and they are not. They are not aware of the source of the tension but know it can be relieved by shopping. The "just-in-case" compulsive shopper is symbolically increasing her sense of control over her world by using buying to be prepared. Prepared for a food emergency, a free-time emergency, or a social emergency. If you are a "just-in-case" shopper, finding a noble excuse for shopping but feeling out of control even as you shop, the first step toward fixing this false fix is to admit to yourself that you are indeed a compulsive shopper.

The Ten Signs of Compulsive Shopping

How can you tell if your shopping is really compulsive? Like any other compulsive behavior, your shopping will be flavored by many of the following characteristics:

1. You may feel *driven* to shop, even when you don't have the time or money.
2. You may feel *tempted* to shop, feeling that it will be *naughty* or *bad*.
3. You may find that your shopping is *impulsive*, that you cannot resist a "sale" sign or store display on your way to somewhere else.
4. You often find that you are *planning* a store visit from the time you awaken, and you center your day around the visit.
5. You automatically *collect* items for shopping lists and consistently feel that you must stop at various stores to be able to check items off on your list.
6. You usually feel *tense* or *anxious* if an unexpected call, chore, or emergency interferes with your plan to stop at a store.
7. You frequently feel *exhilarated* or *gratified* for a short time when you make a purchase. For example:

"When I find something wonderful, I feel like my shopping time was justified."

"Buying something is like getting a birthday present. I feel all happy inside for a day."

"I know this sounds silly, but I shop and shop until I find a sweater or necklace or perfume that has been waiting just for me!"

8. You may feel *guilt* after shopping, and fear that you will be judged irresponsible or bad.
9. You may feel *self-critical* and *punish yourself*, working twice as hard as usual or developing a tension headache, stomach ache, or other stress symptom.
10. You may feel real *regret* and return your purchases— even when they are needed, reasonable, or affordable.

"I feel great when I first buy something. Then the next morning I feel a heaviness in my chest when I think about what I bought."

"I think I'm going to actually change my life with my new look or perfume. And for a few hours I think that it really is changed. Then I get honest with myself, and get angry at myself for being so optimistic."

"You know, I give away half of what I buy so that I don't have to look at the 'evidence' of my crime."

When Shopping Is Compulsive

The three basic elements of compulsive shopping, which are also true of compulsive eating, smoking, drinking, gambling, drug abuse, sexaholism, or even compulsive "telephonism," are:

- a lack of choice about the behavior;
- a short-lived gratification during the behavior; and
- a strong sense of guilt or regret after the behavior.

In fact, according to Dr. Richard Greenberg, president of the medical staff at the Psychiatric Institute of Washington, D.C., compulsive shopping often overlaps with other compulsive quick fixes for women. Why shopping? Because, he suggests, cultural standards and roles dictate that women should be the shoppers. As one of my patients puts it, "If I have to shop at the supermarket for the rest of the family, I might as well shop at the dress shop next door for me!" Why does this quick fix come undone so quickly? Because, Dr. Greenberg suggests, compulsive shopping can be a symptom of more serious problems.

You may be more compulsive in your shopping behavior than you have been willing to admit. Start now by asking yourself how many of these problems you may be trying to avoid by shopping, or deny or block by keeping busy with purchasing.

MARITAL DISSATISFACTION Spending your husband's money reminds you that he is a good provider and helps you keep your disappointment or anger under control.

POWERLESSNESS Making a purchase is making a choice. Buying something, then, may temporarily counteract early non-assertiveness training or current feelings of passivity.

WORTHLESSNESS If your sense of self-esteem is low, you may try to boost it with purchases. "You are what you buy" is what some women try.

BOREDOM Going to a store or shopping mall is a way to spend time when life at home is less than exciting. Stores are designed to be stimulating.

LONELINESS Stores have customers and salespeople. You're not alone when you shop. It's a way of socializing.

A NEED FOR ATTENTION You are waited on in a store. Your purchase is important. You are the focus of someone's attention when a salesperson waits on you and helps you decide. If you feel unneeded or unloved at home, this works as a substitute. To help you find out if you're a compulsive shopper, take this quiz:

The Compulsive Shopper Quiz

Directions: Circle the appropriate number after each question, and add up your score at the end. Do you:

	Never	Some-times	Always
1. Shop to excess?	0	1	2
2. Shop when you don't need to?	0	1	2
3. Buy items you don't need or won't use?	0	1	2
4. Feel guilty about your shopping?	0	1	2
5. Shop when you're angry, depressed, or lonely?	0	1	2
6. Get limited or no pleasure from shopping?	0	1	2
7. Have debts that make your home life unhappy?	0	1	2
8. Hide your shopping from friends or family?	0	1	2
9. Go to work late or leave early to shop?	0	1	2
10. Have a problem with alcohol or drugs when you can't shop?	0	1	2

If you scored between 0 and 4 points, you probably have your shopping under control, although you may be trying to reach for a fast remedy sometimes.

If you scored between 5 and 10 points, you should take a close look at your shopping habits. You are probably headed for two kinds of trouble. First, you are probably not taking the time you need to take care of the underlying problem behind your shopping. Second, you are creating a new problem by compulsively shopping!

If you scored over 10 points, you do have a serious shopping disorder that will not get better on its own. It is time to take care of yourself as you would your best friend, your sister, or your daughter.

Reality as a Remedy

Before you conclude that professional help is necessary, try the following self-evaluation procedures. Each is designed to help you see if you can recognize and manage your shopping behavior. Check each off as you complete the task.

Reality-Testing Your Receipts

Review all of last year's canceled checks and charges in order to determine the exact amount of money you spent on "recreational shopping." As a guide, compare your spending to the following national averages:

Household maintenance (rent, utilities)   35 percent of income
Food, alcohol, cigarettes   20 percent of income
Transportation (cars, commuting, loans)   14 percent of income
Recreation (television, magazines, books) 13 percent of income
Medical expenses   10 percent of income
Clothes, shoes, toiletries
(for the whole family)   10 percent of income

Only 10 percent of the typical family budget goes to clothes, shoes, and toiletries—the category where the compulsive shopper is most likely to see evidence of her compulsion.

If 50 percent of today's working women earn under $12,000 per year, then half of today's working women have only $150 per month to spend on anything beyond the basic necessities. And those who have children and are head of a household—no extra money! If you are in this group and a compulsive shopper, where is the money coming from? Check your expenditures again. If your shopping money exceeded 10 percent of your income, what other area of your expenses suffered as a result? Your vacation plans? Your children's activities or lessons? Your household maintenance? Did shopping really fix more of a problem than it created?

Asking yourself these questions is what psychologists call reality testing. Compare your imagined gains with the real losses you may have suffered. If your perspective on shopping changes, your behavior may change along with your willingness to discover the underlying problems you were trying to fix. If you thought shopping would be less upsetting than direct confrontation of inner dissatisfactions, you may now see that isn't so. In fact, marriage counseling, therapy, or even a weekly massage may be cheaper than your quick fix!

Document Your Daily Shopping

Starting today, keep a shopping diary. Dr. Greenberg suggests that you write down everything you buy and include the time and date of purchase. The more specific you are, the better. Describe how you felt at the time of purchase, who you were with, and what you were doing. Did you have an argument or feel anxious before you went shopping? Write down how much you spent and exactly where you spent it. Did you use cash, credit card, or check?

Then analyze your diary with someone neutral. First, look for a pattern. You can only change patterns after you recognize them. Do the shopping sprees occur at specific times, after specific situations, before upsetting activities or meetings, or in the company of specific people? Do they happen after you've been with anyone in particular? If your answer to any of these questions, or to any you are asking yourself, is "yes," your next step is to substitute a better and more appropriate fix to whatever is emotionally troubling.

If you find you shop when someone has disappointed you, try to tell them what you need to feel better, rather than trying to buy what you don't really need. If you find that you shop before an anxiety-tinged appointment, fortify yourself with thirty minutes of meditation, relaxation, or exercise instead of thirty minutes of heavy damage to your checking account. If you find that you shop to fill time, assess the cost per hour of shopping and spend it instead on lessons, learning, or leisure. If you find that you shop to avoid thinking about upsetting changes in your life, join or gather a women's group instead. You'll be getting and giving help that way!

Beware of Pseudo-Shopping

For pseudo-shoppers, shopping is not the same as buying. Pseudo-shoppers *browse, bargain-hunt, borrow* (by charging), and *bring back* the items—the four Bs. They feel less guilt than the compulsive spender, but in fact they are probably looking for the same instant preoccupations, consolations, and communications for which the compulsive shopper is looking when she shops. If you find that you get a quick fix from pseudo-shopping, treat your symptom before it creates problems harder to fix, like wasting time or interfering with productive activities. Find your pattern and start to practice better management and long-term remedies.

Buying-Behavior Modification

Behavior modification is based on reinforcement. There are two kinds of reinforcement that are effective: reward and the elimination of negative feedback. When either follows a behavior, the chances that the behavior will recur increase. For example, rewarding a child only after she says "please" will increase the chances that she will say "please" the next time. By canceling a punishment when a child says "please," a parent eliminates a negative feedback, and the child is also likely to say "please" again in a similar situation.

How can you use these principles of behavior modification to gain some control over your shopping? Reward yourself with a specific shopping goal after you have succeeded in controlling impulse spending for a week. Pick one item from a list of realistic and justified purchases, and thoroughly enjoy every minute that you deliberately set aside for this shopping. Sense that the activity is under your control and with your own permission. Enjoy the memory guilt-free. Review in your mind each step you took. If you *eliminated guilt* by shopping with deliberateness and by choice, you have now reinforced your controlled shopping a second way—no more negative feedback. Continue this plan, and controlled shopping will win out against compulsive shopping through the double reinforcement you are experiencing.

Remember, until you are fully aware of how you spend your time and money, you cannot change or manage quick fix shopping. So be honest with yourself. Look at your behavior honestly. Only 9.5 percent of American women can afford shopping as a hobby. The rest of us must fix our problems in a less costly and more permanent way! That is not to say that we must never buy on impulse again. But when we do, it should be with the full knowledge of our budget and the consent of our psyche. We can all go overboard once in a while without ruining our lives or labeling ourselves self-destructive.

In fact, as I have stated before, none of the behaviors in this book is aimed at self-destruction. They are all attempts to make something better. Quickly. Privately. Independently. But when your behavior begins to direct you and not vice versa, it is time to fix the quick fix!

FIVE

Quick Fixes

Do you find that you feel cut off, anxious, or depressed when the phone lines are down during a storm?

Do you move furniture the way other women might arrange a vase of flowers? Until the room looks just right? And then change the arrangement again and again?

Do you find that yelling feels good even though you know it's bad? Although you want the fear to fade from your children's faces, your husband's jaw muscles to loosen, and the cat to come out from under the bed, do you yell anyway?

Do you find that you clean while you are on the telephone, while you are going from one room to another, and while you should be getting ready to go out for the evening? That you must clean before you can relax, clean before you can leave in the morning, and clean before you can sleep at night? You have heard that cleanliness is next to godliness, but you know this much cleaning is ridiculous.

Any "yes" answer puts you among the majority of women who have contributed their experiences to this book. After eating and shopping, the most-often-used quick fixes are telephoning, redecorating, yelling, television tune-in, cleaning, and workaholism. A telephone is usually an arm's length or a footstep away. Your furniture is always there to move or paint, work is there to do, the television sits waiting. Yelling takes no planning at all. And cleaning never ends. Why take the time you don't think you have to look inward, when you can just reach out and quick-fix instead?

The Phone Fix

If you want it, it's right there. Ninety-seven percent of American homes have telephone service, according to the American Telephone and Telegraph Company. That's more than 160 million telephones and over 1,200 million miles of wires connecting us to our families and friends. The Bell telephone companies estimate that more than 600 million daily conversations take place over their telephones and another 200 million over independent lines. That's more than 800 million calls a day. I wonder how many are quick fixes?

Most quick fix telephone calls are to mothers, friends, and siblings, in that order, but they are rarely identified as quick fix calls. Women don't call and say, "Help!" They call to get help, but not ask for it. They say, "How are you?" instead, and wait for a chance to say, "Me, too," if the answer on the other end is negative.

"I'm sorry to hear that you're not feeling well. I've been sick, too . . ."

"I know just what you mean. Frank's been very distant lately, too . . ."

"I can hear that you're busy. I've been overwhelmed myself . . ."

Why don't we just come out and ask for what we need? Why don't we say:

"I just called to get some sympathy . . ."

"I'm about to cry and needed to talk . . ."

"I think I'm going to explode if I don't tell you that . . ."

"Please bring me flowers, tonight . . ."

Probably because we are taught to be polite. Inquire after others first. We are taught to be cheerful, to say, "I'm fine," no matter what. We are taught to keep our faults hidden. Don't say, "I forgot," or, "Didn't get to it."

However indirect our approach, we continue to reach for the telephone. There are some "advantages":

1. Telephone conversations permit you to hide your facial expressions and body language. This can be an advantage when we don't want to show nervousness, anxiety, anger, or disappointment.
2. Telephone conversations permit you to do at least one other thing at the same time. Since most women do at least two things at once most of the time, telephone talking lets her feel that she is not wasting time by doing something for herself alone. She is also cooking dinner for the family, or sorting mail for the office, or sealing envelopes for the school committee.
3. Telephone conversations can be cut short more easily than face-to-face visits. If you fear that your emotions are getting out of control or that you want to retreat from your cry for help, just say there is someone at the front door or office reception desk. I know one woman who cuts herself off in the middle of her own sentence by pressing the disconnect button to make the interruption seem like a mechanical failure!

4. Telephone conversations permit you to hide the helping hand at the other end from someone at your end. If you are embarrassed that you still want your mother's permission to take a day off, or if you feel unentitled to call Daddy when you are needing a kiss-fix because you are a grownup, the evidence is gone when you hang up. Your husband and children may never know that you still feel like a little girl at times. Nor will your boyfriend be jealous of your old friend if the call is over when he comes over.

5. Telephone conversations also help you hide other fixes you may be using while you are on the phone. No one can detect alcohol on your breath if you are using the phone. Nor can they see you eating your way into the night. This way, you can mix fixes in secrecy.

Obviously, I was being ironic when I referred to the "advantages" of using the telephone as a fix. Each of these five "advantages" points out a quick fix problem. Our struggle to hide our emotions, for example, may be made easier by talking on the phone rather than face to face, but why should we hide them at all? To whom must we prove that nothing upsets us? From whom must we hide these feelings? Probably from no one. The world does not run like a well-oiled machine, nor do we!

What if our emotions are remembered by our confidants? If they use them against us, they are not good confidants. Use that information about them to select more empathetic and helpful people to talk to next time you need a conversation. When you do have a much-needed telephone talk, please don't be polyphasic. That is a fancy way of saying, "Please don't do two or more things at once!" Practice sitting down and concentrating entirely on the emotions you are expressing, the problem you are discussing, and the response you are receiving. Don't feel guilty. You made the call; now make use of it fully.

95

If you are using the telephone to hide a fix that can be fatal, like alcohol or drugs, or to hide a fix that can compromise the quality of your life as much, if not more, than the problem that triggered it, get off the telephone. Instead, meet with your friends, your sisters, your mother, your father, your spouse, your lover, and seek their help. We cannot do it all alone. Sometimes we need help dealing with our emotions, our traumas, our own personality dynamics, and our roles. Ask for that help. Go beyond your circle to a therapy group or individual therapy if you need it. Make your call for help a real call if you need it.

The Fury Fix

Yell and shout, and let it all hang out? Good words for rock 'n' roll lyrics, bad advice for women—unless they are alone in the car. If shouting, pouting, stamping, yelling, and throwing things around makes you feel better, do it for yourself as an indulgence. But do it when you are by yourself since it is a *private*, personal self-communication. If you saw such behavior at home when you were growing up, then you already know that the yelling fix rarely fixes anything. The following list reviews what the research tells us about this phony fix:

- The more frequently we yell and shout, the lower our threshold becomes for yelling and shouting. In other words, it will take less and less to trigger this response.
- The more we yell, the more *adrenaline* is released into our bloodstream, making logical thought and self-control more difficult. Thus, we are spiraling up into a frenzy until mental or physical exhaustion sets in. If this type of exhaustion is the only time you feel tired enough to finally fall asleep, it is time to change your pattern.
- The more we yell, the more we teach those around us

how to yell. If it seems to work for us, our children will try it. Imitating behavior that works for others is called *modeling*, and it is the most powerful learning process a child is exposed to. That is why abused children tend to be child abusers. Let's try to break that cycle now!

- The more we yell, the better we become at it. This is called the "practice effect." Soon yelling will become the first option that jumps to mind when we are frustrated.
- The more we yell, the more we reinforce ourselves for yelling. If we feel better afterwards, we will try it again. If everyone around us treats us better afterwards, we are doubly likely to try it again. So why take the chance that it will work? Let's reinforce ourselves for fixes that address the frustrating situation and the frustrated feeling that leads to yelling.

Your Yelling Inventory

To change our behavior, we have to understand it first. So let's look at the reasons we may yell. Check all the items that are true for you:

———— I yell most when I have encountered an unexpected interference with my daily routine.

———— I yell most when I have been insulted or feel insulted.

———— I yell most when the people or person around me start(s) to yell.

———— I yell most when I am physically uncomfortable with pain.

———— I yell most when I am physically uncomfortable because of the weather.

———— I yell most when I am premenstrual.

_____ I yell most when I feel that I am being ignored or not taken seriously.

_____ I yell most when I feel I have no choice about something.

_____ I yell most when my expectations are disappointed.

_____ I yell most when I am physically tired.

_____ I yell most when I think I can get away with it.

According to the research of Dr. Leonard Berkowitz of the University of Wisconsin, if you checked at least three, the odds are that they included:

1. Yelling when you feel personally insulted.
2. Yelling when you feel unexpectedly frustrated in achieving a goal.
3. Yelling because the weather is oppressively hot.

If you checked them all, you have found your fix; but go beyond reading. Call a community or county hotline or mental health office and find a support group for women who have trouble controlling their tempers. Outbursts of aggressive behavior of any type are difficult to change, and group methods seem to work best. You will receive understanding, alternative suggestions, actual practice in behavior modification, and reinforcement for new approaches. You will also probably receive the number of a "buddy" to call in case you feel that you are losing control. If such a group isn't available, set up your own group or buddy system, with the guidance of a social worker, psychologist, or psychiatrist.

Yelling Modification and Moderation

To cut back or eliminate your yelling response, examine your triggers. If unexpected events trigger your frustration most easily, then it is your sense of control over your environment or your day that is being violated. When this happens, too many of us blame ourselves for not having anticipated everything in the world that might happen. We then get angry at ourselves, but yell at everyone else in our frustration.

"How could anyone have done something so stupid!"

A much more practical approach when control is no longer within our hands is to accept the situation and give up trying to take control at that point. If you are stuck in traffic, turn on slow music and relax each muscle group in your body in turn. Use the time to unwind rather than wind up. If you are stuck with a disappointment, don't make it into a personal failure. Treat yourself to a new plant instead of planting your feet in the hall and yelling through the house.

If you yell most when you are insulted, your outburst usually means that either you are giving someone else's opinion of you a good deal of weight, or you are seeing that person as diminishing your self-esteem, or the insult is similar to the insults that you direct at yourself. Perhaps all three dynamics operate for you.

"Well, I now know how you really feel about me!"

"How dare you speak to me that way!"

"That's one insult I'll *never* forget."

The first step is to review the importance of the person who insulted you. If it is a bus driver, salesperson, or anyone else who doesn't know you, take their harsh words as information about them, not about you. It means they are in a bad mood, impatient, impolite, or insensitive. Understanding this will not mean that you will be less annoyed, but it will mean that you will take their remarks less personally.

If the person insulting you does know you and is important to you, then you may feel that their insult means you look less than perfect in their eyes.

"I would rather quit than work here if you feel that way about my report."

It may mean that their disapproval is worth listening to. But listen for information about how you come across to others. Don't conclude that all of you is summed up by one criticism, or that your self-esteem need be linked to being "scolded" or "insulted." Your self-esteem belongs to you. An insult reflects someone else's needs or sensitivities. Decide if the insult can be helpful as information or just hurtful. If it is the latter, handle it as just that: a statement meant to hurt, not a fact about you.

If your yelling reaction to an insult erupts because the button someone pushed is the button you don't want to admit that you have, join the rest of humanity. We are all most upset when we are criticized for something we have already criticized ourselves about and tried to hide from ourselves.

"Me? You accuse me of being like her? Never!"

It is usually those very same unacceptable behaviors of which we are least tolerant in others. The mother, for example, who is most critical of her own procrastination will find procrastination intolerable in her daughter. So, get to know your own least acceptable traits—and either accept them or change them. Once you do, the criticism of others will have less impact because they are neither revealing a secret nor adding to your own self-deprecation.

If you yell most when you are around others who yell, you are demonstrating what social psychologists call the "contagion factor":

"Don't raise your voice to me. I can outshout you any day!"

An early French sociologist named Gustave LeBon explained the spread of aggressive behavior among people in contact with each other as the result, in part, of our suggestibility. Social learning theorists like Albert Bandura claim that we yell more when we are with others who yell because we see that yelling works for them and we want to make it work for us, too. Watch out for the contagion factor, suggestibility, and imitation. They can lead us into behavior that we are not actively choosing ourselves.

If your yelling coincides with physical discomfort, pain, hot weather, fatigue, or premenstrual tension, then you are likely not to be taking your discomfort seriously enough to ease it directly, or you are convincing yourself that someone else is responsible for your discomfort—probably not accurately.

"How can you make so much noise without a jackhammer?"

If you are experiencing discomfort, admit it to yourself and take time out to help yourself. If you don't, you will not make good use of your time anyway, since it may be spent yelling.

If your yelling is a protest against feeling that you have no choice about something, review the reality of the situation. Sometimes we of course do not have real choices, but more often, I have found, we do but are reluctant to voice our choice, take responsibility for our choice, or feel that our choice should be known through mental telepathy.

"If you really loved me, you'd know how I felt about that plan."

As I have suggested again and again, take and make every choice that comes your way. The more you fix your feeling of choice and control on a daily basis, the less you will need the yelling fix on a minute-to-minute basis.

The Television Tune-In

A large majority of American households have televisions in them, and it's not surprising. Where else can you find someone who is endlessly amusing? Someone who will talk on and on when we feel like listening and stop talking the instant we have heard enough? Someone who can transport us instantly into the living rooms and bedrooms of other people—and into their personal intrigues as well? The televison can lend a we-are-there feeling to glamorous parties, faraway lands, current events.

Unfortunately, it is possible, even easy, to misuse this magnificent invention. Most television addictions begin with a desire for excitement. Why settle for an afternoon of ironing when you can watch two women throw cocktails at each other as they fight over their two-timing soap opera lover? Why settle for an evening of redundant conversation with a tired husband when you can see a woman just like yourself whoop with joy as she wins a trip to Tahiti on a game show? This kind of television watching is harmless entertainment. Some women also mention that they feel thankful *not* to have lives like the ones their favorite soap opera characters live. It makes them feel glad life's misfortunes are sitting on someone else's doorstep. Other women feel a "How well I know!" kind of kinship with problem-ridden plots. Many women say they enjoy the cheerful situation comedies that come on in the evening because they show views of ideal family life they feel may still be within their grasp.

The soaps also coincide neatly with the daily after-lunch low. It's an ideal excuse to sit down and take time out. Unfortunately, once you've sat down, you may have a hard time getting back up again and continuing with your day. Particularly with soap operas. The soaps are carefully planned to be a hard habit to break. It takes a strong woman indeed not to turn on the set when her heroine's car broke down yesterday in the same town where a rapist is on the loose. Soon you may find that you are canceling appointments so you can be home on time to watch your soap opera (or operas). Normal afternoon activities —cleaning, ironing, shopping for dinner—may be left undone. Or you may be taking a TV into work! Suddenly your life has as many problems as the lives you see on television.

The fantasy of television can also be a substitute for the real people, places, and things in our lives:

> Maureen and Kevin had just passed their seventh wedding anniversary, and Maureen had responded good-naturedly to all the teasing about the seven-year itch. But Kevin *had* seemed more distant lately. Their lovemaking had dwindled to a couple of times a month, and he seemed to be spending more and more time at his job instead of coming home at six the way he usually did.
>
> So Maureen began to watch the six o'clock news. Soon she was looking forward to it, particularly since she had decided that the anchorman was charming and handsome. She caught herself wondering what it would be like to be stuck on a desert island with him. She even entertained thoughts of hanging around the door of the broadcast studio—it was only a train ride away—so she might catch a glimpse of him.

Though Maureen's newfound fantasy love kept her from confronting the painful subject of her relationship with her husband, she wasn't solving any problems either. Her television tune-in was no substitute for conversation or counseling.

Are You a TV Addict?

To find out if your television set occupies too honored a place in your life, ask yourself the following questions:

1. Do you spend more than three hours a day watching television? (This doesn't include watching television while doing other things—tidying up rooms, ironing, fixing dinner.)
2. Do you fantasize about the people and places you see on the set? Do you imagine they are your friends? Do you have imaginary conversations with them?
3. Would you rather watch television than talk to real people?
4. Is television preventing you from getting errands and work done?
5. Do you cancel appointments or rush home because a favorite television show is on?

If you said "yes" to two or more of these questions, you may be addicted to your television! And it's not just a psychological addiction. You may be using the excitement you see as an adrenaline fix to give you energy, or you may be using the mindlessness of some evening television shows as an escape fix. Some research has shown that watching television can relax your body almost as well as biofeedback.

To turn off a TV habit that has gotten out of hand, try the following:

- Schedule important activities outside the house for the hours when you watch the most television.
- Reward yourself with small gifts for not watching television.
- Go to a restaurant or diner when your compelling show comes on. Have a bite to eat or a cup of coffee with a friend who shares your problem.
- The next time the television breaks down, postpone repairs.
- Ask yourself why your television habit has gotten so out of hand. If your life needs more excitement, arrange for some! If your marriage needs help, look for counseling —it may be a painful step now, but it will pay off manyfold later on. If you are so tense that you need television in the evening to help you fall asleep, reevaluate your schedule and do something about it. Try substituting meditation and your own thoughts for the sleep-inducing value of a show that will not improve your life at all.

The Furniture Fix

We laugh at jokes about husbands coming home late and tripping over the sofa, which was someplace else in the morning. We smile when we remember the color we painted our college dorm room or the magazine pictures we permanently plastered on our bedroom walls. We look longingly at photos in decorating books and imagine ourselves in those perfect rooms. We drag home treasures from auctions and from garage sales, and feel as though the new touch has been added to *us* for a few hours.

"When I picture myself in a luxurious room, I feel rich."

"When I drive at night, I try to look into windows to see what colors I like best on walls and what curtains other people choose. Then I pretend to live in that house and see how I feel in those surroundings."

"When I repaint my apartment, I feel like I've freshened up my whole life. I even feel better at work for a while."

Most men claim to be less affected by their surroundings than women. Perhaps because most men are left brain–dominant, and the left brain is less interested in colors and design than in labels, language, and logic. Women, on the other hand, seem to use both brain hemispheres more equally and more frequently. They therefore probably notice the gray walls and lack of windows in the office even while they are adding up numbers or writing memos. As we all know, women have been raised to notice the colors and fashions of furnishings. Their age-old role is "to make a home." When we want to fix up our dissatisfactions with our home, what could be a more appropriate fix than to remake our home?

The fix-up fix is so accepted by our society that there are magazines giving 1,001 decorating ideas each month, and do-it-yourself stores in every city in the country. In fact, I've had women tell me in my private practice that they were considering divorcing their husband because he was not handy enough to help redecorate.

The problem with the refurnishing or refinishing fix is not that the activity is destructive, but that the expectations are too often unrealistic. People who live in perfect homes are not perfect. Women who have feminine bedrooms are not less aggressive than women in industrial-style bedrooms. Red carpets won't lift depression permanently, nor will yellow walls let the sunshine in if your eyes are closed with fatigue or despair.

A second problem with this fix concerns money. Fixing up a room may feel good because you have something concrete to show for your labors and expense, something tangible to point to after six weeks of work. But the money can't be recovered if it is needed, since paint stays on walls and sofas look worn quickly. Redecorating can be expensive. More money is spent by Americans on home furnishings than on liquor, medicines, appliances, radios, or televisions. More on building materials than on bakery goods. More on hardware than on fish and meat and fruits and vegetables combined!

In addition, the preoccupation with your project may succeed in distracting you from the real situations you would like to rearrange—your marriage, your career, or your compromises. The time and money we spend on redecorating often excludes any possibility of spending time or money on marriage counseling, psychotherapy, exercise class, graduate courses, new résumés, or seeking new friends.

So listen to one woman who used to use the redecorating fix:

> "Every time I had the urge to rearrange the house, I'd use that as my clue that I had other rearranging to do. I'd check out the rest of my life, try to put things in order—and *then* I'd rearrange the furniture, too. Still do!"

The Cleaning Machine

Push your button and you clean? Make you angry and you shine silver? Make you frustrated and you scrub tile? Make you sad and you prune plants? Or does it work the other way around for you: Do you find that you get anxious if you don't clean? Do you find you get frustrated if you don't scrub? Do you find that you feel guilty when you don't prune? Either way, you are caught in the cleaning fix.

Although compulsive cleaning is just as rigid and confining a behavior as messiness is undisciplined and inconsiderate, compulsive cleaning is reinforced and rewarded for women. If a woman buries her feelings in scouring powder, she is said to be a saint. If she buries them in a heap of old newspapers, she is said to be a slob.

Robin smoked and owned a parakeet and a cat. Ordinarily, this was not a problem for Robin. But when Robin had a blind date or friend coming to the apartment, the ashes, bird feathers, and cat hair made her wild. Literally. She would start hours before her date or visit and begin to clean the apartment. Not just the offending ashes, feathers, and hairs, but the entire apartment. She would start from scratch. Dusting, vacuuming, glass polishing, furniture polishing, floors, walls, and even the inside of the refrigerator. It was only after she had exhausted herself cleaning that she would be able to turn to dressing and doing her hair for the evening. She was often running too late by then to do as good a job on herself as she had on the apartment.

Robin goes beyond presenting her guests with a clean apartment. She knows she is using cleaning as a fix for her anxiety about a date or visit. She thinks she might be worried about letting anyone into her "private" life, so she keeps her private quarters so immaculate that there are no clues to her faults, habits, or pleasures. Just clean surfaces. When she kept her room that clean at home, her parents always showed it off to their friends. At college, she was proud to be pin-neat. But now, she wonders if the energy she spends cleaning has anything to do with being clean!

Cleaning Compulsions or Cleaning Fixes?

Some women use cleaning to use up their tension, anger, or frustration from the day or week or past. Others, like Robin, find that they are "addicted" to this fix. They actually experience withdrawal symptoms if they try to stop: anxiety, insomnia, irritability. The differences between cleaning as a fix and cleaning as a compulsive behavior are:

- Cleaning as a fix is intermittent. Cleaning as compulsive behavior is repetitive and constant.
- Cleaning as a fix involves variations in what is cleaned and when. Cleaning as a compulsion is ritualized and stereotyped. Like Robin, the cleaner must always start from some beginning point and follow through to the end. Often, if it is interrupted, the ritual is begun all over again from the beginning.
- Cleaning as a fix feels good while we are doing it. Throwing yourself into throwing out old clothes feels better than throwing yourself at your husband with clenched fists and fury. When you are finished with the attic, you feel calm enough to have a good talk with him, perhaps. Cleaning as a compulsion does not typically feel good or pleasurable. In fact, a compulsive cleaner usually has a desire to resist her impulse to clean.
- Cleaning as a fix may lead to inappropriate cleaning. You know, reorganizing your jewelry box at midnight after you hang up from trying to reach your boyfriend for the tenth time that night. Cleaning as a compulsion

109

usually leads to excessive cleaning: cleaning that is unrealistic. Hand-scrubbing a floor, for example, that was just scrubbed and had no traffic.

Controlling Compulsive Cleaning

If your cleaning is a compulsion, it is time to take control of your behavior. That is not to say that you should not keep your house clean, do your own housekeeping, or show off your homemaking talents if you choose to. But choosing to is the key. If your cleaning is on automatic pilot, try the following steps toward self-help:

1. Think back until you can remember when your cleaning rituals began. What was happening then? Had you just gone through a trauma, a loss, or a major life change? Since cleaning can symbolize taking control and fixing up a messy situation, rethink your solution to that earlier problem. Did cleaning bring back old friends after you moved, or clean up the memory of being "dirtied" by a sexual attack, or successfully prevent unexpected news from disrupting your organized world? We know the answer is "no." Admitting this painful insight to yourself can help to make cleaning behaviors less compulsive.

2. If you cannot connect compulsive cleaning to an early trigger, think of your cleaning pattern now. When do you clean—the morning, the evening, Sundays? If you did not clean quite as compulsively, how would you be using this time? Often we find that the cleaning is "saving us" from free time or intimate time or family time. If this is your case, try to confront the issues you may be avoiding by cleaning. If you need help uncovering or confronting them, speak to a therapist or a trained clergy

counselor, or look for a women's group. If your cleaning is so ritualized and time-consuming that your life is in disarray because of it, seek a consultation with a psychiatrist (M.D.). There are new medications that seem to be of specific help in managing obsessive-compulsive behaviors.

Cleaning Up Your Cleaning Fix

If your cleaning is not compulsive, but is a fix that doesn't fix, look for clues to the real problem in your selection of cleaning modes. For example:

If you iron your wardrobe when you are having a rocky time romantically, consider that you may be getting ready to step out with new people.

If you wipe fingermarks from walls after not noticing them for a year and a half, you may be trying to eliminate evidence of someone's presence.

If you suddenly decide that the inside of your closet must be reorganized, ask yourself if you really want to reorganize any of your inner feelings.

If you are polishing your silver and crystal, do you want to entertain more or feel surrounded by opulence?

If you are cleaning out the refrigerator, are you ready for a diet?

Since non-compulsive cleaning usually leaves us feeling as if we have accomplished something with our extra adrenaline, most women say they are not very troubled by this fix. If that is your feeling, I suggest you keep cleaning. At the same time, I suggest that you know why you are cleaning when your cleaning is a fix. Then you can have the clean house and solve the real messy problem also! If you would prefer to give up extra cleaning as your fix, remember that dishes left to air-dry have fewer bacteria than dishes wiped with a towel, and an unmade bed can be seen as airing out.

The Woman Workaholic

Cleaning up our desk, cleaning out the in-box, and clearing up messages at work seems to be a quick fix for many of us when we are feeling at loose ends. Like rearranging a closet or scrubbing a floor, tearing into work can burn up adrenaline, distract us from personal and family problems, narrow our world to a specific task, and offer us a chance to accomplish a sense of closure and completion.

Being a workaholic doesn't necessarily mean that you will score high on the Fast Pace Scale, but it is very likely. If you are a perfectionist, editing students' papers late at night will help you feel a part of the imperfect world has been put in place before your bedtime. If you are a stimulus junkie, taking on more projects than you have time to complete assures you that you'll have no time to dwell on depressing or unsettling thoughts. If you are tired of attending to the emotional needs of your family and friends, work is a noble escape. If your parents gave you consistent approval for the work you did in school, you may be seeking the same kind of approval from your boss or yourself.

Having a baby was something Terry had looked forward to for years, but when the baby finally came, Terry found herself regretting intensely having quit her job. She got a better job at better pay. And although many people were amazed that she could handle a career on top of motherhood, she was not. Her "work" was no burden. In fact, she loved it so much she often stayed extra hours if she could arrange it with the sitter. It was so quiet in the office. And so neat, after the messiness of childbirth. And so clean, compared to all the spills and accidents that are part of being a mother of a small child. Terry especially loved working at her computer. You could always predict what it would do. She enjoyed handling the color-coded disks, which all had their places in color-coded boxes. Most of all, she enjoyed thinking adult thoughts, which she would exchange with her colleagues the next day.

For Terry, work was the antidote to a disorderly life over which she felt she had little control. She was lucky enough to get her fix five times a week, plus praise from her friends and family, plus a salary!

When to Worry About Work

In a society that is built on the work ethic, it is sometimes very hard to see the line between work and too much work. Fortunately, today's managers and employees are also more health-conscious than ever before, and the link between work and various physical ailments—stomach ulcers, eczema, back trouble, even heart attacks—is fairly well accepted. It is only a matter of time, I believe, before the psychological aspect of overwork will be something everybody can talk intelligently about. I think that the women in the workforce may be the ones who bring this about. The brigades of young mothers who want to be with their children but must work for either financial or psychological reasons have already to begun to speak out about balance.

What are the psychic costs of workaholism? They are several. One is stress that spreads outward from you to your children, your husband, your parents, your friends. Or you may become depressed, particularly if you feel you have no control over your workaholism. If you are a stimulus junkie who loves to feel crazy-busy, you may find that every now and then you crash in exhaustion and have to call in sick. For most people, these are the predictable consequences of poor time management and a lack of balance. You are using work as a fix, and fixes can be fixed at home, by you.

If stopping work or slowing down produces anxiety, insomnia, or irritability, the problem may run deeper. Working may be a compulsion. The differences between work as a compulsion and working as a fix are:

- Working as a fix happens now and then, as you need it. Working as a compulsion happens every day, all day, and into the night (or starting very early in the morning).
- Working as a fix involves variations in the kind of work and when it's done. Working as a compulsion is as ritualized and stereotyped as compulsive cleaning. For example, a woman with a compulsion to work might start every day by looking through her in-box from top to bottom and placing things in neat piles. If she is interrupted, she feels a compulsion to put everything back and start over.
- Working as a fix feels good while we are doing it. Knocking off a pile of letters that need answering brings a certain satisfaction as the pile grows shorter. Working as a compulsion does not typically feel good or pleasurable. A woman caught in a work compulsion may even feel miserable as she approaches her work for the day.
- Working as a fix may lead to inappropriate working—for example, labeling folders in a file that no one ever uses. The idea is that the work is therapeutic, and it doesn't matter if it's useful! Working as a compulsion usually

leads to excessive working: offering to complete huge jobs due the next day that you have no chance of completing without staying up all night. The woman using work as a fix doesn't *want* to stop; the compulsive worker *can't* stop.

If your workaholism fits the pattern of compulsive working, you will probably need outside help to break the pattern. Consider a psychotherapist—a psychologist or psychiatrist—now, before you lose your health or even your job.

Help for the Workaholic

As with any of the quick fixes, the first step is recognition. Are you really overdoing it? The way to find out is to look inward: Are you exhausted? Are you depressed? Are you having lapses of memory or slips of logic due to lack of sleep? Have health problems cropped up lately? Is your work—the very work you feel is so important to you—suffering because you are tired, sick, or sick and tired of your area of endeavor? No one—I repeat, no one—wants you to do these things to yourself. You should not want to do them to yourself, either.

Now look outside yourself, to the people around you. Are you asking others to take more than their share of household responsibilities in your absence? Are you expecting too much of your children? Do they seem to want to be with you more of the time? Do your best friend and mother complain that they never see you? This is not to say that you should be everything everyone else wants you to be. But you should listen to these signals that say the balance in your life may be off a little or a lot.

Now take a look at the work you do. Are there jobs you do that don't really need doing—little things? You may enjoy these because success at them is guaranteed, unlike the raising of children or the making of a marriage! I know one executive woman who sneaks in early to fill the coffee machine because she knows it is one of the few things in her day that she will complete and complete correctly, that will not be controversial, and that no one will criticize her for!

If you are doing extra work, ask yourself why. Often the reasons are those elusive feelings of success, control, and closure. Problems like these can vanish once you've identified them and tried to work them out. If they don't disappear, look for seminars and workshops on employee health, efficiency, attitude, time management, and similar elements of the working life. Some of them involve going away to a rustic, isolated camp or beautiful conference center for several days. Many are paid for by charities, business groups, university centers, or outreach programs. If you feel such a seminar is absolutely and totally out of the question, you may need it more than you think.

In all cases of workaholism, you will have to take your problem in hand yourself. Don't count on your boss to do it for you!

SIX

Big Fixes

Marriage, remarriage, divorce, maternity, and moving are big life changes. Instead of being true decisions about our futures, the big moves can be attempts at fixing up our old lives. Sometimes they work, sometimes they don't.

> Jan moved to Chicago with her husband after he was fired for the fourth time. She thought they'd make a new start. They bought a new mobile home and Jan became pregnant for the first time. Everything seemed rosy for a while, as Jan's husband worked hard, inspired by the baby. But in her eighth month of pregnancy he was fired again. She now had her old problems with money and her marriage, plus a new baby on the way.

Jan's solutions didn't work for her because the problems she was trying to fix were beyond her control. Her husband's problems on the job could not be fixed by a move or a baby.

Christa's problems were more suited to a big fix:

> Christa has been unhappy since the day she married. Burt was sweet and good and kind, but not someone she felt that she loved. She convinced herself he would make a great

father for her children. He was reliable and would always take care of her. But Christa was still unhappy. She felt that her one life to live was not being spent the way she wanted to live it. She divorced Burt although the rest of the world wondered why.

She remarried quickly. Her second husband had a child already, was less successful, and certainly less adoring. But Christa was happy. She laughed more, entertained more, and soon had a baby of her own. "I know it doesn't seem to make sense," she'd say, "but in real life this works for me."

Mending with Marriage

We so often confuse weddings with marriages, houses with homes, and children with motherhood that it is no wonder we often think happiness begins with "I do." We forget or never realized that marriage is a commitment to live your life with a particular other person. That is all. If the other person is not someone you can live with, there is no marriage. Marriage is not an altered state of consciousness, or a magical kingdom you enter enchanted. It is daily work. It is daily dealing with your own problems plus new ones. The daily and nightly pleasures come only with that particular other person you married. If the two of you do not develop your own patterns of play and responsibilities, the marriage can't even fix loneliness. Women may turn to marriage for a number of fixes:

- Young women may want to resolve their identity struggles by becoming Mrs. So-and-So.
- Teenagers and women living at home may want to escape their parents' supervision and authority.

- Many women want to fix their financial life by finding a second income or a fiscal father image.
- Some marriages are statements of rebellion. For some women, the choice of partner reflects that she wants to break out of tight religious or social confines.
- Soap operas tell us women may marry to fix that rebound feeling. Sociologists and psychologists suggest that it's true. When our esteem is low, we choose partners less carefully and fall in love more easily.
- Older women are more likely to marry in order to fix loneliness. But it's the relationship, not the institution, that really fixes this problem.
- Women often say they need to be needed. Unfortunately, when they marry needy men, they usually end up with much more to fix than they bargained for.
- Don't dismiss social pressures as a reason for marrying in the 1980s. Perhaps we are no longer old maids at twenty, but by our thirties we may find that our social friends have moved into marriage and we feel left behind.
- Likewise, wanting a baby is often a woman's first motive for marriage. For these women it is the biological clock, not the social clock, that is ticking too fast and needs fixing.
- Wanting companionship and emotional security may be fine fixes provided by marriage—so long as your partner can meet those needs.
- Some women tell me that they like being a wife. They see domestic chores, cooking, and child rearing as their job of choice, and marriage as their employment contract.

Unfortunately, marriage is less available for some age groups and less stable for others than ever before. This makes marriage less likely to work as a "fix" for women than ever. Most men do not think of marriage as the way to sex or food these days. Both are available in the open market, though AIDS is causing us all to rethink our lifestyle choices. Even women who offer extraordinary physical attractiveness know that they may find that they are being "traded in" for newer models in a decade. As for children, "his, hers, and ours" are the norm now among the remarried set. Children are no longer a marriage bond.

Marriage as a big fix, then, usually doesn't work very well. Unless a couple is relatively compatible in age, socioeconomic background, and attitudes, the kind of relationship that will give us security, role definition, and companionship may not develop or last. We are at least one step ahead if we first develop our own sense of identity and support networks. Then we can look for a partner at leisure and bring more to the relationship when it does develop.

The Divorce Fix

Women who are thinking about divorce as a way to fix general dissatisfaction echo these thoughts:

"I think I'll trade in what I have for someone even better"; or

"I never had a chance to be young, so let me try it since my teenagers seem to love it"; or

"I think I'd rather be alone than in this marriage"; or

"I'd like to do it all again, so I think I'll start again"; or

"If I wait any longer, he might leave first"; or

"If I wait any longer, he or I might get sick and then we'll be stuck together."

Divorce as a quick fix for a frustrating or difficult marriage may be somewhat less frequent than ten years ago, according to statistics, but seems still to be the popular path. No-fault divorce laws relieve us of some of our guilt about not working things out. Religions are more lenient about their stand on divorce. Our families and friends are no longer shocked—or are divorced themselves!

The Realities of Divorce

The rule of thumb on divorce as a remedy for a difficult marriage seems to be this:

- If you would rather be on your own than with the man you are married to, try separation.
- If your fantasy is that you will trade in what you have for a more perfect fit, think twice. Unless there are clear-cut issues such as cruelty, mental pathology, or deliberate alienation, which signal the need for divorce, women often find that what they have is better than what they might get.
- The pool of available men is never as promising as when you are still relatively young. Such men are not yet encumbered by ex-wives, negative histories, and children.

The Reasons for Divorce

If you would like to compare your marital complaints against those of almost five hundred divorcées, here is a list prepared by Dr. Stan Albrecht and printed in *The Journal of Marriage and the Family* in November 1979. The problems are listed according to how often they were offered as a reason for the failure of a first marriage.

Infidelity
No longer loved each other
Emotional problems
Financial problems
Sexual problems
Problems with in-laws
Neglect of children
Physical abuse
Alcohol
Job conflicts
Communication problems
Married too young

Despite a decade of popular literature suggesting open marriage, open communication, and delayed commitments as pluses, we can see that loyalty and love still rank as the top requirements for an enduring marriage.

When we do decide on divorce as the fix for an unfixable marriage, what can we expect? A readjustment period that may be difficult even if we wanted the divorce. We will not socialize the same way:

"A divorce really shows you who your friends are versus who had been inviting you to dinner just because you were on his arm."

We will not have company and someone to talk to (or yell at):

"Some of our best conversations were in the middle of the night, when we would both be restless and unable to sleep. We would hold each other and really talk about the important things. I never thought I would miss those moments as much as I do."

We will not parent the same way if we have children:

"Now that Jack isn't around as much any more, I find myself worrying intensely about finding male role models for the boys. I hope they'll be willing to stay in the Boy Scouts through their high-school years."

Typically, we have residential custody of children and must continue to parent with our ex-husband for much of our lives:

"A clean break? No such thing when there are kids involved. We still fight, about their schools, friends, and spending money. At least he goes somewhere else to sleep."

Legal fees are very high, as is the expense of reorganizing a lifestyle:

"My fantasy about finally doing all the things my husband was too stingy to do went up in smoke when I was hit with the lawyer's bill."

And deciding how to handle dating and postmarital sex is complicated:

"All the issues I struggled with as a teenager are back. How far should I go on the first date? How much responsibility for preventing pregnancy and disease is shared? When do I introduce someone to the family?"

The Other Side of Divorce

Women who are divorced and have not remarried are not regretful, as a rule. I was amazed to find that most of the women surveyed did not regret their divorces, even if they had wanted to remarry and didn't. Those who remarried said their new marriage was for the most part as difficult in new ways as their old marriage was difficult in the old ways. It was their greater willingness to work at the marriage that most said led them to more satisfaction the second time around. Those who had not remarried, though they had wanted to, still said:

"I don't want him, you can have him!"

They would, indeed, rather be alone. As one woman put it:

"A good marriage beats being alone. But being alone beats a bad marriage any day."

Once again, we see the choices we can make and chances we can take. Both marital and divorced happiness takes work. Divorce is not a fix that comes with a replacement warranty or a happiness guarantee. Make your decision slowly and carefully.

Divorce Decision Guidelines

When is the urge to divorce a fix for a difficult marriage? Be careful if you are reaching for the fix:

- When your marriage difficulties coincide with important life changes or crises that would upset you even if you were not married. Too often, we may blame our spouse for anxiety and tension that reflects our own life passages.
- Before you have tried counseling or therapy. A third person may help you see that you are personalizing a spouse's reactions to his own life crises or his own life history, and help you develop some perspective and even sympathy instead of anger or hurt.
- Because you have had a better offer. To some men, we are most attractive when we are unavailable, and vice versa. The divorce fix for general unhappiness seems to be fading. Since two incomes have become more of a necessity than a luxury, and tales of friendly divorces have turned out to be mainly tales, give yourself and your new relationship enough time to test your feeling toward your current spouse, explore your own issues, and seek counseling before you give up and move on.

The Remarriage Rescue

Try this true/false quiz to see how much you really know about remarriage:

1. _____ Most people who marry a second time will marry a third time as well.
2. _____ Most remarriages are between divorced people rather than a divorced person and a never-married or widowed person.
3. _____ Fewer than 50 percent of American children are living with both their natural parents.

4. _____ About 80 percent of the million people who divorce each year will remarry.
5. _____ Remarried women rate their happiness higher than never-divorced married women.
6. _____ Child rearing, not sex or money problems, ranks highest among the remarriage problems.

Let's review the answers and learn about remarriage as a fast fix for divorcehood.

1. False. As of a few years ago, only 2.5 percent of American adults marry more than twice.
2. True. Most remarriages are among divorced people. In fact, the older divorced woman has a higher rate of marriage than the widowed or never-married woman of the same age.
3. False. At least 65 percent of American children are living with their natural parents in an intact marriage. About 10 percent are living with one natural parent in a remarriage.
4. True. Since almost 80 percent of the 1 million divorces this year will lead to remarriages, we can expect to see about 30 percent of next year's marriages be remarriages.
5. False. Remarried women do not rate their new marriage as happier than their old marriage. In fact, many studies suggest that remarried men and never-divorced married women report the most life satisfaction. Does this mean remarried women do not have as good a selection of men the second time around as they did the first time, that they settled, or both?
6. True. Child rearing does seem to be the most difficult problem to fix in second marriages. The authority of the step parent, the visitation of the natural parent, and the mix of new children all need continual readjustments.

Perhaps the biggest difficulty women claim to face in re-marriages is the lack of norms, expectations, and social guide-lines. They must each write and rewrite their own script for this new form of family living. If that kind of challenge is just right for you, consider the remarriage fix. If you know that you are more comfortable within a stable extended family, a predictable course of life events, and a defined set of expect-ations, don't reach for this fix too quickly. Change is not the equivalent of improvement. And a fix is not a fix unless something is broken. So check out the relationships you have very carefully before you decided they are beyond mending.

The Baby Boom

In many languages, there are many sayings about babies that tell women that having a baby can fix up most problems:

Babies bring their own good luck.
A house with a baby is a happy house.
Give a man a son and you will be his wife.
Give birth to a daughter, and you will be a mother for life.
Babies at play make all cares fly away.

In truth, most mothers can tell you that most babies at play give her time to do the dishes or laundry! Since parenting and home-making are not high-status jobs in this society, what does having a baby fix?

"Having a baby gave me constant companionship. I laugh with the baby and even nap with the baby."

127

"My baby helps me feel like I am contributing to my family's heritage. My parents are old, and I wanted them to see their grandchild."

"Before I had a child, I felt that my life was too lopsided. I was all brains and no heart. Now my career is balanced by real life."

"I felt left out of the female parade without a baby. Now I'm marching like everyone else—and it's fun!"

"I was always afraid that I'd be unable to have a baby because I had had two abortions. I'm so thrilled that I was wrong now that the time is right."

Our next question is, What happens when having a baby is a patch for problems? This is a very important question since having a baby involves a lifelong commitment. If you are motivated by a problem at just one point in time, how happily will you cope with the needs of the child throughout all other points in time?

The number-one reason for trying the baby fix, according to the women surveyed for this book, was to make a marriage into a family. When many women felt that the glow had left their mate's eyes or that his eyes had begun to roam, they became pregnant. Most stressed that they wanted the child anyway. Did this fix work for them? Usually not. They usually had their child and husband problems, too. On the other hand, they said that they may have cared a bit less because they were now busier, had company, and knew their husbands would be their child's father even if he left the marriage.

Just as marriage can be an identity fix, many women said they used motherhood to define themselves. "All I ever wanted to be was a mother," I often heard. For some women, becoming a mother means they no longer have to feel like someone's daughter. They have now gained adult status in their own eyes. For teens, this may mean a premature motherhood. For other women, becoming a mother adds a new identity to her many others. Women who decide to have a child in their mid-life passage say they feel like they are starting over again, but this may mean a lifetime of fatigue and little free time ever.

Most women agreed that the baby fix did not affect their marriage at all the way they thought it would. They agreed that it ended the honeymoon flavor of the marriage and that most of their husbands competed with the baby for attention. No matter how much their husband loved the baby, he still showed some resentment, they agreed. The husbands wanted to play with the baby, eat dinner, and then relax in bed and make love the way they used to. Try to meet those needs after a day with the baby full time or a day split between work outside and the baby in the house!

Does that mean that motherhood is not a marriage fix? Yes. Of course it can be a rewarding experience for its own sake. It can add a new dimension to a bonded marriage and shared responsibilities to a marriage now on a two-career track. The key is to make a joint decision about parenting. Unilateral decisions can provide only unilateral fixes.

The Moving Fix

Every year, about 17 percent of the population in this country moves to a different house or apartment (U.S. Bureau of the Census). About 35 percent of people in their twenties move, 20 percent of those in their early thirties, 13 percent of those between thirty-five and forty-five, and one quarter of the population of Washington, D.C. Although many of us are moving for jobs, education, and climate, many women are moving to try to fix a bad situation with a new location.

About 18 percent of women in this country are single. Why would they be moving? Like Laura, many are moving to find men or more money:

> Laura had lived in Boston all her life and had gone to college there, too. She had been engaged there, had broken her engagement there, and now was feeling overwhelmed with memories. It was in Boston that she had had her first date and attended her best friend's funeral. It was there that she had spent cold winters and summer-school summers. Laura decided that her melancholy needed fixing. She tried to fix it by moving to Florida. Now she had warm winters, hot summers, rainy springs, and the same memories. She had a new boyfriend but still found she had to go through a recovery period from her last love.

With the population of women I surveyed, a much larger percentage of women said they moved than the national average reflect. Perhaps that is why many were attending the stress management conferences I teach.

The married women who said that they tried moving as a big fix for their big problems report that the fix was not generally successful. If they moved to put distance between themselves and their mother-in-law, they often found their husband's dependency or guilt problems moved right along with them. If they moved to put distance between themselves and their own parents, they often found that they still needed some face-to-face therapy to work out their own separation difficulties or conflicts. If they moved to provide their children with a better school system or climate or quality of life, they often found that they had succeeded but at a price. New neighbors, new networks, and new doctors are hard to find easily, and the woman of the house must usually do the finding!

Most of us do not realize that change, even positive change, taxes our energy reserves. We must handle unexpected emergencies. We are stuck in the middle of a big commitment, and there is usually no turning back for a while. There are more adjustments than we can know ahead of time and less familiarity to fall back on. Life changes raise our risk of ulcers, depression, and even the common cold, according to most research. Our immune system, it seems, may be compromised by the constant activation of our fight-and-flight system during moves and readjustment periods. Soon our reserves are figuratively and literally exhausted.

Divorced women move more frequently than married women. The reasons are many. Some are forced to move to fix their financial situation after the divorce. Some are forced to move to leave an area that has unhappy associations. Some are forced to move because their house is being sold as part of the settlement or because they are rejoining their parents or original community. Some are just forced to move.

Does moving away after a divorce fix anything? It didn't for Debbie:

Debbie had lived in Texas for twelve years of her marriage, although she had grown up in Oregon. After her divorce, she wanted to mend her disappointments by moving back home. She took her five-year-old boy and moved back to the community she had grown up in. She felt a great relief to be home again. For about two months. Then, she says, she found that she wanted to go home again—to Texas. Her mixed feelings confused her for a while. Then she realized that Oregon might have been her original home, but it was so no longer. It was a nice place to visit, but she didn't live there any more. Debbie returned to Texas and slowly rebuilt her life.

There are no quick fixes for big problems or big changes. But sometimes a move can be part of a big fix-up project:

Pat was married at nineteen and had her first child by the time she was twenty. At thirty-three she felt weary. She wanted to do more than manage the framing business that she operated from her basement workroom. She had ignored her husband's affairs, since she preferred to avoid having sex with him anyway. When he announced that he had fallen in love with his latest girlfriend, Pat thought that she would be only too happy to see him go.

She was surprised that she missed just knowing another adult was around. She was surprised that she no longer wanted to socialize with her "couple" friends as a single. She was surprised that she felt embarrassed retroactively about her husband's infidelities. And she was surprised that her children and framing business now seemed more than enough to keep her busy. Her dissatisfaction had really been with her marriage.

Pat decided to restructure her life. She moved to the neighboring town so that she could keep her clients, keep her children in the same parochial school, but start a new group of friends and date without self-consciousness. For Pat, the move worked.

The other group of women who often reach for the relocation fix are the 10 million widows in the United States. Understandably, many do not want to run a house on their own. Many more cannot afford to keep their homes or apartments after their husbands die. At least 40 percent of men die without leaving their wives enough money to continue their life as it was. Many widows must move to survive. Some move to residential communities for the aging, some to family, some to the Sunbelt to avoid heating bills and expensive winter clothing.

Any move is difficult, particularly if it is without choice. A forced fix will create sadness, resentment, a sense of loss of control, and a depression born of powerlessness. Familiar and comforting routines are broken, territory and terrain are different, status is altered, and autonomy is usually diminished. For those widows who can afford to stay in their homes after their husband has died, I advise them to wait at least six months to a year before making a decision about moving. Moving is never a fix to be undertaken lightly. It may be more overwhelming than the memories or realities of staying.

The group of women in my survey who speak most often about using moving as a big fix are married women in their thirties and forties. One in five women in the group reported that they had moved at least once for no other reason than to try to fix up their emotional lives. They do not move for their career, their children, or financial reasons. Nor do they move to a faraway place. Many said they thought a new project would cheer them up. Some hoped to feel more important in an impressive house. Five said they hoped to tie up their husband's time and money in a move and, therefore, tie their husband closer to the marriage and farther from the divorce courts. Three said they moved just across town, but up three or four notches in the local social ladder by doing it. One said she moved so that she'd be in a better bargaining position in case the marriage failed; another moved to a house she wouldn't mind living in alone in case her husband left. Most moved at a time when they felt a lull in their marriage and equated a more solid house or apartment with a more solid home and relationship.

To Move or Not to Move

Does the moving fix usually work? Since most of you have at least one story about a couple who bought a bigger house or apartment and then separated within the year, our first guess would be "no!" Most of the women in the survey also said "no!" If the marital problem really centered around lack of space or commuting time or community facilities for sports or education, the moving fix would theoretically work. The more common truth is that if the problem centers around communications, intimacy, or power struggles, a new or different place to live does not change those big issues. In fact, moving often accentuates such problems, while adding daily hassles and major inconveniences.

Think twice and then once again before reaching for this fix!

Make sure the remedy you choose is appropriate for the problem you have. If it is not, redefine your problem and your fix. If your move is basically a new project to distract you from a problem that needs working out, or a relationship that needs working through, or a loss that needs mourning, wait. First work through your problem, relationship, or loss. If you then decide on your move, it will be a decision, not a fix. And if you then decide to move—enjoy it.

SEVEN

Secret Fixes

"What are your secret fixes?" I asked over one thousand women as I lectured across the country. "Just jot them down on a piece of paper, and I promise I won't read your list until I get home." What did I find when I read through the notes? Fantasizing, masturbating, having sexual affairs, napping, and gambling, in that order. I expected to receive notes saying that a quick bite of chocolate, an emergency telephone call to a sympathetic friend, or an extra cocktail before dinner was the secret fix that kept most women going for just a few more hours when they were out of patience or strength. But no. Fantasizing, masturbating, having sexual affairs, sleeping, and gambling were the fixes they were trying to keep secret.

The first question we must ask ourselves is why these are the fixes that we must keep secret. Maybe because they are usually seen as male fixes. Think about male fantasies. They are made public and legitimate by magazines, movies, ads, and jokes that are shared at meetings and sports matches.

- Think about a man taking a nap in the afternoon. Would he be embarrassed about it? Probably not. He'd be likely to tell everyone with pride that he had taken

135

time for himself and felt he was entitled to it. And he'd be right!

- o Think about a man masturbating when he felt aroused —in the shower, for example. Do you think that he'd be likely to think about that fix as unusual? Doubtful.
- o Think about a man who joins the office football betting pool, bets on a softball game, or plays poker for money every Wednesday night. Would he be likely to hide his losses or his winnings? Particularly his winnings? No. He'd be likely to rub it in if he won and expect sympathy if he lost.

These are fixes, then, that we may be keeping secret because we think that we are not supposed to use them—they are male fixes in this society. This, in turn, creates not only the problem of shame among women who find these fixes, but also the problem of inaccessibility. If these fixes are not discussed, not admitted to, and not even acknowledged, how can they be assessed or helped?

This is the key to the whole paradox. In fact, it may be that *because* these behaviors are usually so completely self-serving, pleasurable, and assertive, women are particularly uncomfortable with such fixes. Often the fantasies, naps, masturbation, or gambling are far from troublesome fixes. These fixes become problems only when they seem to take on a life of their own and begin to control our life.

Some fixes, like napping, may be a true comfort and valuable fix. The problem is that many women feel shame when they take time out for themselves. Sharon is one of those women:

Sharon gets up with her family, makes breakfast for her husband and three children, sees them off, and then checks on her mother-in-law next door. Next she puts the laundry in the washing machine and makes all the beds except hers. After putting the washed clothes in the dryer, Sharon gets back into bed. She sets the alarm for 11:30 A.M. and turns off the phone. She tells everyone that she was out doing errands or gardening, or with her mother-in-law. By noon, her children are home for lunch and Sharon is rested but feeling guilty—so guilty that in five years of napping she has never told anyone about it. Even in sharing the information with me, Sharon warned, "Don't use my real name, please. I'd be so ashamed if anyone knew what I did."

Sharon's nap is a wonderful example of a quick fix that is appropriate for a quick problem. It is only her own guilt that creates difficulty for her. Barbara's fix is also a natural behavior that became a problem for her only because of her embarrassment about it:

Barbara enjoys working with her husband, living with her husband, and having sex with her husband. Every once in a while, when he spends a weekend with his brother, she enjoys masturbating. She says it is a different kind of experience than making love. She says she likes the solitude and personal privacy. But her husband doesn't know. "He'd think I don't need him or love him. Or he'd think I was crazy!"

Barbara doesn't know that masturbation is a normal response to sexual impulses. It is a lifelong capacity and characteristic of females as well as males. Sometimes we masturbate for the pleasure, sometimes for the tension release, sometimes to remind ourselves that we are not solely dependent on others for our inner needs, and sometimes as part of a dreaming, falling-asleep, or waking-up state. Sometimes we don't know exactly why we feel like masturbating, but we do. After masturbating to orgasm, many women feel relaxed, while others feel energized. Unfortunately, many more seem to feel guilty.

Games of chance, too, make most women feel guilty. Instead of games, they become fearful omens of a disastrous and shameful loss of control.

> Roberta loved to play the state lottery. She would buy a ticket each week and fill in the boxes differently each time. Sometimes she would use the birthdates of all her nieces, nephews, sisters, and brothers. Sometimes she would spell out names converted into the number of the alphabet that each letter represented. Sometimes she would fill in space to form a pattern. And sometimes it was just hunches and random picks. It was always fun while Roberta was doing it, but always painful afterward. She would leave the stationery store as if she was leaving a den of vice. She felt foolish for thinking she would beat the odds, and foolish for having spent her money on gambling.

Roberta, like many other women, has set up a controlled, legal, and potentially exciting gambling game to pep up her week. She is not risking money for necessities, and the games give her something to look forward to. Some psychologists suggest that the excitement of gambling can act as a mild antidepressant. Some suggest that it is an extension of childhood competitions. Others think that it is natural human risk-taking behavior being expressed. They are probably all correct to some degree. What is important is that playing the lottery is not Roberta's problem. The *meaning* of gambling bothers Roberta. To her, it means being foolish rather than risky. Being out of control rather than security-minded.

Sorting Out Secret Fixes

If you have a secret fix you feel guilty about, it is time to review the behavior. If your behavior is not creating a new problem or not serving to obscure a problem, it is time to stop feeling guilty. The guilt will create problems: self-blame, self-consciousness, and self-centered obsessing. This doesn't mean that you need to share your secret with the world. It is no one's business how you take care of yourself when you are alone. If you masturbate, nap, or like gambling games, you are not alone! If you have a secret passion for a soap opera, or slide the *National Enquirer* into your grocery purchases when your neighbor isn't looking, or stash candy in the glove compartment, or save your old love letters where your husband will never find them, you are one of many.

When should you worry about your secret fix? When your time, energy, or thoughts are becoming consumed by it. When the rest of your life revolves around it. When you awaken obsessed by thoughts of your next bet. When you can't concentrate on the here-and-now because you are fantasizing or being-in-love in the there-and-then. When your nap becomes so important that you begin to get anxious at the thought that you might have to miss it on some days. Then you are no longer fixing a problem. You are creating a problem or masking a problem that must be examined before your attempt to make things better actually makes things much worse!

Fantasizing is an example.

The Fantasy Fix

The fantasy fix becomes a problem only when it interferes with our enjoyment of the present or our assessment of reality. It is

139

a fun fix when it is an extra added attraction in our life. It's a problem fix when it preoccupies our daily life.

Some of us try to fix the present by retreating into the past or running ahead into the future. If we are insulted, tired, or overwhelmed now, memories of summer camp, bedtime stories, or Grandma's hugs pop up from the past. If we are frustrated now, broke now, or lonely now, we find that images of what might be still to come can occupy us for surprisingly long stretches of time.

> Whenever a salesperson was rude, a bank clerk brusque, or a neighbor unfriendly, Suzie would fantasize about her next acting role. Instead of a small part on a daytime soap opera, she would have a major part on a nighttime, prime-time series. Then she would be recognized. Then she would be treated differently. Then her neighbors would hope that *she* would be friendly.

What prime-time celebrities might tell Suzie if they had a chance was that rude, brusque, and unfriendly people are not worth fantasy time, nor should they be a motivation for a career success. They are people who should not be taken seriously in the here-and-now—and certainly not in the future either. And success doesn't insulate us from unpleasantness.

Even more important than the particulars of Suzie's story is the general theme. We miss much of the present when we live in the past or future that life seems to slip by. Women spend so very much time focused on another's needs and meeting them quickly and quietly that to spend our own time in the there-and-then or past-and-when is a double waste.

Why We Fantasize

Dr. Fritz Perls, founder of Gestalt therapy, suggested that we fantasize to gain closure. He suggested that by nature we do not like to leave unpleasant, confusing, or upsetting situations as open chapters. We want to close the book on events and relationships that we don't like. As a result, we recreate negative situations from the past again and again in order to make them turn out differently this time. Or we fantasize about negative current situations coming out differently in the future. Either way, the closure is all in our heads, and the negative situation is in the here-and-now. Isn't it better, he suggested, to solve the problem in the here-and-now than to spend our time living in other times?

To follow his advice, we must first recognize when we are recreating unfinished business from the past. If we lived with people who wouldn't let us get a word in edgewise when we were young, recognize your tendency to drift toward the same kind of people now. If you do, it is probably to try to prove that you can get a word in edgewise as an adult. But was it worth all the effort? And did you really fix the original problem, which now only exists as a memory or old fantasy?

And if you find that you spend much of your time trying to fix the present by fantasizing about what you could or might say in the future if you were ever to bump into that ex-boyfriend or college professor or former boss, are you really fixing anything? Just recall how often you may spend time fantasizing about what you should have said during your last fight with your husband that would have given you the last word. Does that change the way the fight really did end? Your last word would have given you closure, and you miss it!

Sometimes the clue to the problems we are trying to solve

141

through fantasy comes to us through "head-humming." During research I did for *Glamour* Magazine, I found that most women find that a melody can be trapped in their head for hours and hours. This phenomenon is what I call "head-humming." Sometimes the melody serves only to block upsetting thoughts from coming to mind. Sometimes we hum for closure, since we shut off the radio a few bars before the end of a song and we must finish it—and finish it and finish it.

But more often, the words to the song, even when we can't consciously remember them, echo the problem in the present that needs fixing. Songs about running away to join a circus, about being on a chain gang, or about how we'd be missed if we were gone can certainly tell us that we are feeling overused or underappreciated. Melodies that have love themes are not head-hummed by coincidence only. Listen not only to the melodies in your head but to the words that go with them. You may be surprised at what you learn about yourself.

Fantasies, like dreams and fairy tales, are not meant to be scripts for real life. Hopes may be. Goals may be. But fantasies are usually fixes.

- They may compensate for what is missing right now.
- They may elaborate on a part of your life that you particularly like.
- They may distract you from conflicts that cannot yet be settled.
- They may even permit you to experiment safely with a wish or fear. In fact, they seem to function in order to permit you to go on with your daily life, the way dreams permit you to stay asleep when a dog barks by weaving the disturbing sound into your dream.

The Problem with Fantasy

Although fantasies will tell you much about your life, it is your life that may need readjusting, not your fantasies that need acting out. Fantasies are often exaggerated, dramatic, and inappropriate in order to make their point to your busy and preoccupied mind. Women who act out their fantasies as prescriptions for life instead of examining them as sources of clues about the conflicts in their lives very often find that they have traded one side of a conflict for another. Instead of having achieved a fix, they have accomplished a dilemma.

> Ellie fantasized about being a career woman. She taught part time, but fantasized about telling people at cocktail parties that she was Dr. Ellie or Professor Ellie of the History Department at State University. She loved her two daughters but craved a title other than Mom.
>
> Ellie might have interpreted her fantasy as a clue that she needed to be mentally challenged, to be with adults more, or to have status other than through her husband. Instead, she took her fantasy at face value. Rather than working her needs into her current life, she left her life. She left her daughters with her husband, enrolled in a doctoral program, and set off to be a historian. She tried to "do over" her life, instead of starting from where she was. She finished a master's degree but found that she couldn't afford to go on for a doctorate on the salary she was getting as a part-time teacher. Once she became a full-time teacher, she could no longer have the time to complete her studies. She missed the girls, fought with her husband for custody, and found that acting out a fantasy was not the same as working through a problem.

143

The story of Ellie is not unique. I hear similar stories in my private practice. Popular magazines encourage couples to act out sexual fantasies rather than to understand them as private visual clues to personal feelings, often from the past. A rape fantasy, for example, might mean a woman wishes to feel no responsibility for her sexuality. Instead of understanding this as a clue to her guilt about sexual impulses, she may act it out with her husband and then feel humiliated, terrified, or angry. Or she may fantasize about other men. This fantasy may dilute her fear of making a commitment to one man while permitting her to do just that. If she believes her fantasy is a script rather than a fix, she may hurt her husband's feelings and confuse her own by telling him about her fantasy or even acting it out.

The moral? A fantasy is a fantasy is a fantasy. Use your fantasies as clues to what needs fixing from your past or in your present. If you find that the fantasies themselves are becoming your daily fixes, try to focus on the here-and-now and address your problems before your free time becomes time lost in thought. If you find that your fantasies are becoming your scripts, remember that you must start your future from where you are now. Try to work out your problems by making yourself as important as everyone else in your life, not by throwing away everyone else in your life as Ellie did. If your fantasies, however, are passing fancies that make you smile, enjoy them. Your imagination can be more than a small comfort.

The Sex Quiz

Although sexuality is as natural as fantasizing and as feminine as sensuality, we often think of sexual outlets as male tension reducers. We expect the teenage young man to be sexually active. We expect the wealthy husband to have affairs. We expect the older widower to be deluged with available women. We even encourage our sons, brothers, and fathers to remain sexually active. Too often, we have our own double standard for ourselves, our daughters, and our mothers. Try this true/false quiz and see how many surprises you encounter:

1. _____ No more than one in ten of our grandmothers had secret affairs.
2. _____ Although men usually have about six nocturnal erections, women do not show signs of sexual arousal during sleep unless they have an erotic dream.
3. _____ Although men can show sexual arousal (erection) within a few seconds of stimulation, a woman takes significantly longer to lubricate.
4. _____ More young boys masturbate than young girls.
5. _____ Most married women stop masturbating.
6. _____ Most women who have extramarital affairs do so to get revenge against their husbands.
7. _____ The overall pleasure of sexual affairs is reported as greater than marital sex for women.
8. _____ Non-married women today are as interested in recreational sex (one-night stands, casual partners) as men.

Here are the general guidelines for your answers:

1. According to Alfred Kinsey's famous survey, more than one in four of our grandmothers were having secret affairs!
2. Patricia Schreiner-Engel, Ph.D. at Mt. Sinai Medical College in New York, finds that women do lubricate during their sleep cycles and not in response to dreams necessarily.
3. Almost all physiological studies report that women can

begin to show signs of arousal (lubrication) within three to ten seconds of stimulation.

4. Shere Hite in *The Hite Report* tells us that much more than half of the 3,000 women she surveyed have masturbated.

5. William Masters and Virginia Johnson in *Human Sexuality* report that more than half of married women masturbate into their older years.

6. Pepper Schwartz and Philip Blumstein tell us in their book *American Couples* that even women who have affairs usually believe in monogamy, and they have affairs most often when they are emotionally dissatisfied in their marriage.

7. Most women still prefer sex to express affection and love rather than just "fooling around."

8. Non-married women are concerned about all sexually transmitted diseases since most have a more hidden and consequential impact on the female reproductive system than the male system; that is, fewer early symptoms and thus more damage before diagnosis and treatment.

Go back over your answers to the true/false questions. Every answer should be false!

What Does Secret Sex Fix?

This quiz demonstrates that women are indeed sexual. The "secret" is out. But not all sexual behavior is tension-reducing, although some women do use sex as a quick fix for nonsexual impulses, tensions, or needs. When we do, the real problem remains unfixed. The most frequent problems that are not fixed by secret sex are loneliness, pleasure deprivation, low self-esteem, fear of dependency, and dissatisfaction in a relationship.

Boredom

Maggie's most recent attempt to feel good about herself involved "falling in love." She was married, but felt lonely most of the time. Falling in love gave her fantasies—dreams that she could watch in her mind's eye while her husband watched football and baseball on television. She and her lover had sex whenever they could. She felt like a teenager again.

Then the lover explained that he owed his wife his life, that he would never leave her. Overnight, Maggie lost interest in having sex. Her undying passion died. Her desire for her lover left. She watched her husband watch television and felt lonely once again.

Maggie was trying to add excitement to her life, compensate for her husband's lack of attention, and prove her attractiveness by reaching for a sexual affair. Since all three motives were not primarily sexual, sex could not really answer her needs. She temporarily blocked upsetting thoughts about her tuned-out husband, but after her fling was over, she was still left with her problem. And some guilt besides.

Fear of Dependency

Sally wanted to marry Paul. She pursued the relationship with as much interest as he did—until he became interested in marriage. Her dream-come-true became a nightmare for her. She would awaken feeling depressed each morning, and found that her depression lifted only when she had sex with other men. She told herself that she was not ready, that she was not sure, that she was not committed. She had been through this three times before and knew better. She suspected that she was using sex with other men to prove to herself that she did not have to be dependent on Paul for her sexual needs—or any other needs, for that matter.

Sally's quick fix for fear of dependency was sexual independence. At the same time, her dependency needs were as real and as natural as her need for self-sufficiency. She was in conflict and "acting out" the two sides of her conflict over and over again. First she would get involved, and then she would pull away. Then she would get involved again, and then she would need her freedom.

Instead of acting out her conflict, Sally needed to work it out, to find a compromise, not a quick fix. She had taken the first step by acknowledging to herself her own pattern of sexual sabotage with Paul. She had to work hard to be honest with herself and Paul about her fears of commitment in the future.

Insatiability

Jenny said most people treated her sexual problem lightly, but for her it was not a joke. No matter how frequently she had an orgasm, she would not feel satisfied. She felt obsessed with sex. She didn't tell her boyfriend that she was masturbating a few times a day. She sensed that her insatiability was frightening him. The same thing had happened again and again. She felt out of control and frightened herself. She had heard the terms "oversexed" and "nymphomania," but did not know if they were treatable conditions. She knew that she was a sex addict, but didn't know why she was or how to change.

"Sexaholics" are, indeed, addicted to sex. They feel anxiety as a withdrawal symptom, and only another fix of sex reduces their anxiety. With every sexual fix, their behavior is reinforced since they feel better for the moment. Although men who fix all their tension with sexual release are usually referred to as "studs," women who reach for this quick fix are considered sick, "easy," or weak.

Actually, both men and women who try to make things better this way are invariably making things worse. They are vulnerable to sexually transmitted diseases and impersonal liaisons. Either through mislearning or through a predisposed disorder, sexaholics confuse all feelings of tension with feelings of sexual tension. Since tension is a part of most daily life, sexual cravings become part of their daily life as well. First, they must learn to discriminate between the various types and sources of tension they feel, and then they must practice alternative ways to reduce non-sexual tension. This is best done in support groups, like Sexaholics Anonymous, in biofeedback programs, at large teaching hospitals, or in private psychotherapy.

Fear of Homosexuality

Gerry panicked at the thought of a Saturday night alone. She went to an all-women's college, but managed to date every weekend and use the neighboring all-men's college library to study. She became engaged twice in graduate school. By the time she was twenty-five, she had been involved with more than thirty lovers. She preferred living with a man to dating him, but was afraid to marry because she knew that she would soon want to move on to another man. She knew her urgency about being sexually involved with a man was interfering with her selection process and her planning process. She suspected that her urgency was really anxiety provoked by same-sex fantasies. She worried that her fantasies meant she was homosexual.

For Gerry, sex with a man temporarily fixed her fear of being a lesbian. Since her fantasies emerged even during sex with a man, the fix did not last long. Her withdrawal symptom was anxiety.

What Gerry did not know was that same-sex fantasies are so common among women that they are considered part of a norm. Women in this culture are raised by women; stroked, caressed, breast-fed, and rocked by women. Girls and grown-up women kiss each other hello and hug each other when they meet. When women want gentleness, familiarity, mothering, or childlike naughtiness, they often fantasize about sharing pleasure with other women. These fantasies can compensate for maternal deprivation, whisk away self-consciousness about cellulite, or provide an imaginary vacation from performance anxiety. If they are particularly disturbing to you, as Gerry's were, talk about them with a qualified sex therapist or psychotherapist before you invest years worrying, watching, and waiting.

Secret Sleep

Beyond the nap, which is our small comfort or our sensible antidote for fatigue, is the sleep that is *somnambulistic withdrawal*. This term refers to a basic and primitive defense against problems that feel overwhelming. The withdrawal is a retreat into sleep when we are frightened, conflicted, or angry.

Infants have few other defenses against the world other than crying or sleeping. Adults have many, but we don't often exercise them. Instead, we may retreat to this early quick fix.

But women usually feel guilty about this type of behavior when they use it. We are constantly reminded that our grandmothers had nine children, baked their own bread, and ran the family store too. We watch our spouse's eyes close and mouth drop open in a snore to avoid talking about a promise he made three months ago, and we nod knowingly. But when we find our eyes closing during a discussion that is difficult for us to handle, we fear we have diabetes or a sleeping sickness. After all, aren't we always supposed to be on call?

Rather than becoming embarrassed by increased napping, when it is not a sign of a physical condition, a woman can use this quick fix behavior as a barometer of her anxiety, anger, or frustrations. On an airplane, somnambulistic withdrawal is a blessing. Hours and air pockets turn into sweet dreams. On the ground, somnambulistic withdrawal leaves us right back where we started before our nap. The fix doesn't fix our problem, it just postpones it. Sometimes the withdrawal increases our sense of being helpless, childlike, or weak when we are confronted by problems.

Avoidance Sleep

Julie's mother was waiting for an answer. Which week was Julie planning her annual summer visit to Maine? Julie didn't want to visit at all this year. Her mother had a new husband, and Julie did not want to watch him walk around her father's territory. But she missed her mother; her father even more. She would decide to call and set a date, then feel that she needed to lie down for a few minutes first. The few minutes would turn into a few hours of sleep, and then it would be too late to call that evening. The next day she would be too busy for the call, and the next night she'd again be too tired to deal with the decision.

Eventually Julie's mother called her, and the date was set. Her conflict, however, continued, and even when she was in Maine, she slept late most mornings and napped every afternoon. After the visit, her stamina seemed to return, and her need for a nap disappeared. Until her mother's visit to her the next Christmas.

Eventually, Julie will have to mourn the death of her father and find a way to accept her mother's new life without feeling overwhelmed and running away through sleep. To tell her mother that she had mixed feelings about her new stepfather was unacceptable to Julie. She felt that she should carry on as her mother had, should get along with her mother's husband, and should be a big girl about it all.

Depressive Sleep

Over and over again we see that we reach for quick fixes when we are trying to carry on as we think we should. Our "shoulds" are too often unrealistic or unlikely. Our fixes are too often helping us maintain our "shoulds" myths. Each fix leads to the need for another. When the fix is secret sleep, a pattern of withdrawal and napping can be leading to or masking the beginnings of depression.

Allie wanted a baby. She and her husband had tried every method of conception and had undergone all the tests recommended. She had begun to take an afternoon nap so that she would be sure to be awake when her husband came home at night, particularly during her ovulation period. She had begun to take a morning nap because she was so tired from getting up at the crack of dawn to check her basal temperature before she jogged.

Soon it became clear that she would not be able to conceive naturally. She stopped taking her temperature and scheduling sex around her ovulation but continued to nap. In fact, the frequency and length of her naps increased until she stopped selling insurance part time and stopped making dinner at all. When her appetite also seemed to stop, her husband insisted that she consult a psychiatrist.

Although Allie felt she should be able to deal with her infertility, she was not able to. She needed to work out the meaning of being infertile with a professional therapist. She needed to understand that her napping was just one sign of a depression that needed treatment. After Allie was no longer depressed, she still found that she liked to nap. It was not a daily occurrence any more, but was a delightful and delicious rest.

Studying Your Sleep Patterns

If your napping is escapism, ask yourself what you are trying to escape from. If it is yourself, a nap won't work! If it is an escape from the noonday heat, tired feet, or a nagging backache, try it. Sleep cycles and patterns are very sensitive indicators of mood. Pay attention to the following guidelines:

DECREASED NEED FOR SLEEP:
Irritability
Manic episodes (unrealistic expansiveness)
Amphetamine or steroid side effects

Infatuation
Agitated depression (early waking)
Anxiety
Bereavement

INCREASED NEED FOR SLEEP:
Depression
Excessive guilt
Post-traumatic stress (general sleep disturbances)
Adjustment difficulties (within three months of stressor)
Low self-esteem
Relationship stress
Sexual difficulties
Anger (expressed passively by sleep withdrawal)
Sedative, tranquilizer, or alcohol abuse

If your sleep patterns change dramatically for more than a few days, check with your physician and with yourself. Find out if your mind or your body is reacting to a problem with a sleep remedy that may be inappropriate or a warning sign. Do not, under any circumstances, self-medicate yourself for sleeping disturbances, or you will be at high risk for the most dangerous sleep fix problem of all—sleeping pills. Without careful medical supervision, they can too easily lead to addiction, disturbed sleep cycles, and overdose. If this has become a problem for you, read the section on sleeping pills in Chapter 8, Fixes That Kill.

The truth about transient sleep problems is that they usually clear up when you get tired enough. If you are exercising, eating nutritionally, and not feeling mood swings or disturbances, don't worry about the exact number of hours you sleep. Your need for sleep fluctuates with your daily and monthly body temperature and hormonal cycles, and with age. The older you are, the less sleep you generally need. So if you are living longer and sleeping more, ask yourself if you are bored or depressed. And if so, fix the real problem!

Secret Gambling

Earlier in this chapter, we were looking at gambling games that women play with no harm beyond their guilt. Scrabble for nickels, gin rummy for dollars, and the lottery each month for five dollars. If we believe that this is men's play, we'll feel secretive even if we are gambling for dried lima beans.

Daytime television acknowledged women's interest in betting and gambling through game shows, which are the hottest format in syndication. Who is watching these shows during the day? Women! Who is Dialing for Dollars, spinning the Wheel of Fortune, and tuning in to Celebrity Sweepstakes? Women! We not only seem to like betting and guessing, playing hunches and going with gut feelings, but we seem to be quite good at it.

At some point, we all know, the fun becomes a fix. At that point, it is already too late to fix the fix easily. At that point, the new problem has often begun to overshadow the original problem it was meant to treat. Gambling is as addictive as a drug. In fact, it is druglike in that it stimulates biochemical reactions in the body that can leave us with withdrawal symptoms when we stop. The adrenaline has flowed, the endorphins have increased, and the sugar metabolism has climbed. When the gambling is over, we feel drained and depressed. We need another fix.

The gambling quick fix is a serious addiction. A compulsive gambler cannot resist the impulse to gamble away her money, even if it disrupts or ruins her personal and family life or career. A vicious cycle erupts, because when faced with intense personal problems, she gambles even more. Normal functioning becomes impossible. Complicating all of this is an increase in state-sponsored lottery games, off-track betting, dog racing, and casinos.

The compulsive gambler usually starts gambling at an early age, as a quick fix for a variety of emotional ills such as anger, anxiety, or a feeling of deprivation. The roots are deep. A list of predisposing factors follows:

1. Loss of a parent at a young age. This could be from a parental death, desertion, separation, or divorce. This early loss might teach us to feel familiar with gambling losses.
2. Child abuse or inconsistent discipline by a parent, leading to self-abuse through gambling.
3. Exposure. If your mother or father or a close relative gambled when you were an adolescent, they acted as your fast fix models.
4. Inappropriate value placed on material or financial symbols by your parents, leading to lust for fast wins.

The National Council on Gambling describes gambling as a progressive behavior disorder. It may begin innocently as with other fixes—as a pastime or an adventure when it's nothing but fun and excitement with frequent winning. During a losing streak, the bettor is compelled to go on, hoping for a big win to make up for the loss. That's when the problem begins to develop. Even after losses are recovered, the gambling continues. As more money is drawn upon, eventually the compulsive gambler cannot meet her debts, may borrow from illegal sources, may engage in fraud, and could end up arrested. Then comes what psychologists call the desperation phase, when life has little or no meaning.

There are an estimated 8 to 10 million compulsive gamblers

in the United States. Of those seeking help, at least 10 percent are women. To be a compulsive gambler, you engage in the activity at least twice a week. Usually, you are bright and highly energetic but also moody and irritable.

Are you at risk? Answer these questions "yes" or "no."

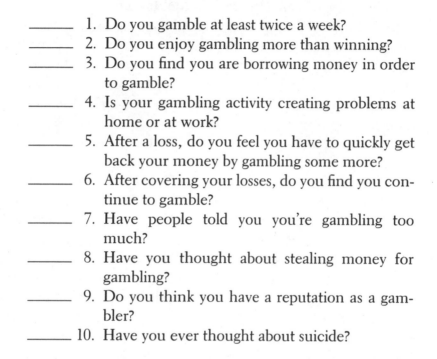

     1. Do you gamble at least twice a week?

     2. Do you enjoy gambling more than winning?

     3. Do you find you are borrowing money in order to gamble?

     4. Is your gambling activity creating problems at home or at work?

     5. After a loss, do you feel you have to quickly get back your money by gambling some more?

     6. After covering your losses, do you find you continue to gamble?

     7. Have people told you you're gambling too much?

     8. Have you thought about stealing money for gambling?

     9. Do you think you have a reputation as a gambler?

     10. Have you ever thought about suicide?

If you've answered "yes" to at least three of these questions, you may be a compulsive gambler.

How do you stop? Compulsive gambling can't be cured, but it can be stopped. A change in attitude toward life in general is required. The feeling that you can't control your own destiny and that everything is predetermined leads to the general outlook that life is a game. The euphoria in placing a bet overrides all other things. But that can change. Once you know that your betting is controlling you, the rest may be easier.

The first thing to do is realize your gambling is a quick fix for something you feel is lacking in your life. Many former compulsive gamblers say they had little or no self-esteem, and the highs they got from gambling replaced those negative feelings with small comforts . . . at least temporarily. Many women gamble to escape something at home: It could be an unhappy marriage (married women who gamble compulsively are often found to have husbands with problems such as drug or alcohol abuse), or boredom, or the stresses of running a household alone (in the case of divorce or separation). Though loners can hide their problem from others, often only with the help of other people can their problem be resolved. It may take time, but it's important to understand what drives your compulsion.

> Rita says her life was one big lie. "I lied about losing money. I lied about where I spent my free time. I was not a good mother to my kids, and I certainly wasn't a good wife to my husband." But Rita blames her husband for getting her started on the gambling habit. "He would get drunk, and I needed to get away. So I'd go to the casino, where time would melt . . . and I'd think about nothing but winning. And if I lost, I'd have to stay longer than I planned, and I'd spend more than I planned, sometimes writing checks to get more money . . . and leaving myself without enough to pay for necessities like food. My sister would often baby-sit for my two children at that time, and eventually she found out what I was doing, and I agreed to look into a self-help group. I'm glad I did. Now I feel like a new person."

Education and support groups, together with counseling, have been found to be the most effective methods of help. One organization that provides this help is Gamblers Anonymous. It has chapters all over the United States and is based on the same principles of treatment used in Alcoholics Anonymous: you share the experiences of other compulsive gamblers and come to terms with the driving force behind your behavior. After taking personal stock, you can start solving problems, put your finances in order, and develop better relationships with friends and family. And then throw away the dice. Life is chancy enough without our tipping the odds against ourselves with gambling!

Uncovering Secret Fixes

We may call them small comforts, minor passions, quick fixes, or common compulsions, but if the behaviors that are keeping us going are secret behaviors, they must not be ignored. Any behavior that we keep secret is a behavior about which we feel embarrassed, guilty, frightened, or concerned.

Start dealing with your secret fix by taking it out of the closet. Examine it closely and honestly. Is the fix really a good fit for your problem? A nap may be a good fit if you need an hour's rest between two jobs, but not if your sleeping is interfering with your daytime activities or nighttime relationships. A betting card game may be fun if it's part of a social night, but it is not fun if gambling is affecting your finances, your concentration, and your control over your life.

If you find that your secret fix looks less harmless in the light of day than it did when it was locked away from your examination, begin to reach for control over the fix immediately. Admit your dependency on your secret fix to yourself. Keep a record of your secret activities for at least a week so your view of your behavior will become more realistic. If you can then identify the need it seems to help you meet, take this need out of your secret closet also. Examine your real needs as honestly as your secret fixes and you may be able to find a solution

159

that will not leave you feeling embarrassed, guilty, worried, or concerned about your behavior. If you can't find a happier solution to your problems on your own, share your secret with a professional. Sources are listed in the back of this book. Help yourself to real help now.

EIGHT

Fixes That Kill

Betty Ford, Elizabeth Taylor, and Carrie Fisher—to name just three—have helped us acknowledge that millions of women medicate themselves privately so they can continue to perform publicly, socially, or sexually. They may medicate themselves in order to make things better, but know they are making things worse.

Alcohol is one of the most popular drugs women use to quietly fix their problems. Domesticated drugs like nicotine and caffeine, recreational drugs like marijuana and cocaine, and abused drugs like amphetamines, tranquilizers, and sleeping pills are also self-prescribed by millions of us every day. How can I say that taking these psychotropic (mood- and mind-altering) drugs are attempts to make things better? My interviews with hundreds of women who are drug-dependent, drug-addicted, or drug-abusive tell me the same story. The original reason women reached for these fixes was to try to function in a way that they believed was *normal*.

If a woman felt depressed, tired, or discouraged, she might reach for a stimulant like nicotine, caffeine, amphetamines, or even cocaine. These uppers, she hoped, would move her from the low-performance range to the *normal* energy or mood range. If she felt too anxious, irritable, or tense to function with the self-control she liked, she might reach for a sedative-hypnotic like alcohol, sleeping pills, or tranquilizers in order to alleviate the tension enough to function well.

Women expect themselves to function at optimum level all the time, whether they are too low from fatigue or depression or too high from tension or anxiety. Once they find that coffee can propel them through a day of twenty priority activities or that alcohol can ease them through an evening of unvoiced conflicts, they will reach for these dangerous resources again and again. Often, the real problem of depression or anxiety is not addressed because it is not recognized or labeled. Sometimes women feel unjustified or unentitled to them. Sometimes the problem is that we make such unrealistic demands on ourselves that we need to resort to drugs and alcohol to live up to our standards.

Janet was finally forty. She had viewed that birthday as a landmark for a decade. By forty, she had decided, she'd be happy and in control of her life. But now she was forty and far from her goal. She was very unhappy with her marriage and felt the demands on her were draining her. Her husband, though successful, kept tight reins on household money, and she had to work in order to buy herself a car. Her pre-teen daughters were both being tutored and needed chauffeuring. She ran from her job as a secretary in a real-estate office to the supermarket and then home to her daughters to drive them to their lessons. She'd then cook until it was time to run out and pick them up again. She wanted her house to be ever clean—and so it was. She wanted her girls to be well dressed—and so they were. She wanted her marriage to seem happy—and so she drank.

Janet would have a glass of white wine while she prepared dinner, and another as she set the table after picking up her girls. When her husband came home, they'd each have a glass, and then another or two with dinner. She'd sip some more as she cleaned up, and she didn't care that Jack would watch television until he fell asleep. Since she'd started sipping wine, the fights about money had stopped. So had her resentment of his lack of involvement with their girls. Life was nicer this way. Now that she was forty, she'd have to make do. She was tired of greeting him with tears and fears. Besides, her morning coffee and cigarettes got her up and out in the morning.

For Janet, optimum functioning meant going through the housewife, mothering, and working-woman motions day after day. She wasn't sure that she was entitled to any appreciation of what she was doing, since she'd seen her mother live the same way for years without complaining. She was certainly unaware of how dependent upon alcohol she'd become until she had to stop drinking in order to take an antibiotic. Within three days she was taking her sister's Valium to get through the evening without feeling panicky and claustrophobic!

Drug Vacations

Women reach for one of the psychedelic drugs, such as marijuana, LSD, and hashish, because these drugs have their primary effect on the sensory system. What we see, taste, feel, smell, and hear is altered or heightened. These drugs are called *psychotomimetic* because they mimic psychoses. A *psychosis* refers to a break in reality, and the drugs offer the promise of a vacation from reality. A promise of better sex without sex therapy. A promise of better communication without self-examination. A promise of a "time out" without much time off.

Although these drugs are often described as non-addictive (unlike most stimulants, tranquilizers, and sedatives), they lead to dependence. When we're addicted, we feel pain or discomfort upon withdrawal—*after* we stop using the drug. When we're dependent, we feel discomfort or psychological pain *until* we take the drug. That is, we're sometimes taking a drug "just in case" we might need it. Sometimes "just for pleasure." Sometimes because we're "in the habit." Soon the fix needs fixing because present time becomes blurred and our capacity for memory becomes impaired.

Millions of women boost their energy, soothe their tension, or make their world more friendly with drugs, but the catch is that many of us are seduced before we realize what's happened. Using our drug of choice makes things better, even if for only a while, and it's not easy to question those rewarding moments of optimum functioning. We don't even want to know we're trading our own good health for them!

Lucky indeed is the woman who finds out in time that her fast fix is fast becoming a fatal fix. Many of the women I interviewed were at this point, and it was a pleasure seeing them trade in the safety pins that had been holding together the gaps in their lives for real mending. These women were ready to understand the fatal fixes they turned to for comfort. They were ready to make things better—*really* better.

Alcohol: The All-Purpose Hand-Holder

Alcohol is the perfect all-purpose hand-holder, because it works so many different ways for so many different women. Who is the typical female drinker?

- The young career women who wants to relax before a speech?
- The married woman trying to feel what she used to feel when she and her husband first started dating?

- The newly divorced woman attempting to get into the mood for a party?
- The older woman desperate to numb the tuggings at her heart that come each time she passes the bedrooms where her sweet babies slept?

They're *all* typical.

Amy had been taught that "good girls didn't," and even after some sexual experimentation in her single years, she felt she couldn't ever really let go and enjoy sex. She had never dared to ask her parents if boyfriends she brought to their home could sleep in her bedroom because she knew what the answer would be. Even after she was married, she had felt funny about sleeping with her husband when they visited her parents. At home alone with him, it hadn't been much better—she'd found it very difficult to respond sexually to her husband's advances.

Now that she was divorced, Amy found herself in a world where she felt more pressure than ever to be sexually free. Her quick fix? Half a bottle of wine—or more—melted away her inhibitions and made the night bright. Eventually one of her fun-loving companions asked her to marry him. A happy-ever-after ending? Not really. Amy still had some problems: What would she do in the morning when her new fiancé wanted more intimacy and she just wanted an aspirin? And after they were married, how was she going to drink enough every evening without his knowing how much it took?

Amy had discovered one of the most common reasons that women use alcohol: to release inhibitions. The ethanol in alcohol literally numbs the central nervous system, first depressing memory, intelligence, caution, and self-control. For women like

Amy, who still can't break the rules her parents made for her so many years ago, or for women who want to escape from a divorce, a parent's death, a child's leaving home, or any other life stress, a drink or several can bring freedom. Among the triggers the experts have pinpointed that push a woman toward alcohol:

LONELINESS More than 19 million American women have lost their husbands through death or divorce. An equal number have never been married. A total of nearly 13 million American women live alone, according to the U.S. Bureau of the Census.

LOW SELF-ESTEEM Society still tells girls that aggression, assertion, and achievement are undesirable. When these girls grow into women, this learned "femininity" combined with a fear of failure prevents them from setting goals and going after them. They learn to take vicarious pleasure in their children's and spouses' successes; they do volunteer work or orchestrate social events rather than compete with men in the workplace. When they do join or reenter the workforce, it's often for lower pay than their male peers.

SEX-ROLE CONFLICTS Though men have been challenged in the last couple of decades to learn how to change a diaper at home, to give a woman equal status at the office, and to expect that she may decide to say "no" at the end of a date, women have had to go through relearning as well. Most women over twenty-five are exploring new role options without role models from the previous generations. Often they end up more confused about their role than modern men. Some modern sex-role conflicts:

- The single woman who phones up her male friend for a date because he said he likes assertive women but finds he is clearly uncomfortable when she does.
- The single woman who can't quite accept the number of lovers she's managed to accumulate over the years.

- The married woman whose husband encourages her to initiate sex but avoids her when she does, or is impatient.
- The woman who leaves her high-paying job and position of power to stay home with her new baby and finds no support system or social status for her choice.
- The woman who *keeps* her job and puts the baby in day care, but experiences constant guilt or even regret.
- The woman whose mother shows a low-grade scorn for her working daughter's casual housekeeping or for her promotion because she is not yet married.

FEAR OF FAILURE In our society, little girls don't get the same kind of encouragement to take risks that boys do, and as a result many of us are afraid to try and afraid to fail. When we do have to try—more than 9 million American women are heads of households, and that doesn't include 13 million women who live alone!—the feeling of insecurity may be one we can barely bear. With financial fears, job pressures, and children to worry about, these women are discovering pressures that men have known about for years, but they're less practiced in dealing with them.

So, like men, they turn to alcohol. Of the approximately 12 million alcoholics in the United States, roughly a third are women.

Alcohol makes these women feel better about loneliness, low self-esteem, sex-role conflicts, and fear of failure—fast. Alcohol enters the bloodstream quickly and is in the brain doing its relaxing act within a few minutes.

The Releasing Factor

Not every woman who feels a need to relax ends up drinking too much or becomes a practicing alcoholic. There may be another ingredient in the recipe for out-of-control drinking: a genetic predisposition—an "X factor" that makes drinking a pleasure. A row of women sitting side by side in a bar can have entirely different reactions to identical gin and tonics. One woman will get sleepy; one will start to feel uncomfortably woozy halfway down the glass and stop. Another one won't enjoy the experience—she'd rather be in control. But one will get turned on, talkative, glowy. She's the one who will have a second, maybe a third, maybe more. It's all a question of how well it works for her.

Unlike a woman who finds that alcohol works for her and begins to use it to laugh, to keep going, or to bear up under pressure, some women will become familiar with an effect of alcohol called "the releasing factor." For your best friend, a few drinks may dissolve fears; for you, they may unleash them. Drinking may help your friend relax under a budget inquisition by a tight-fisted husband; for you they may release a plate-throwing, fist-pounding anger you've stored up and held in all day.

Fran's pregnancy had been a surprise to them both. Although Fran was only too glad to quit her low-paying job at the mall, the baby's arrival put an end to her dream of going back to college. She busied herself at home, making a career of creating meals for very little money and sewing all her clothes and the baby's instead of buying them.

Jack wasn't quite so content. Now that Fran wasn't working, his mind was crammed with worries: How would they ever afford a house? Did Fran really need to buy all that material? And, secretly, he was jealous: Why should Fran stay home all day when he was out trying to sell, sell, sell? He began stopping off for a few drinks on the way home, and soon Fran was fortifying herself for his arrival with rum and Coke.

Every time Fran drank, she felt a growing rage boiling up inside her. Trapped! And he had the nerve to criticize what she was doing to help them struggle along! If only she'd been able to discipline herself at college and graduate! The baby became an irritation, and one night after drinking she threw a plate at Jack. The next night, she threw a glass and called him a bully, a loser, and several unprintables. By the third night they were both frightened.

For other women, this "releasing factor" unleashes sexual drive or sadness. And that's just the beginning of the snowball that alcohol sets rolling down the hill. After alcohol disrupts a woman's memory, intelligence, caution, and self-control; after she forgets errands, misses meetings, spends too much at the department store, has a fender-bender with the car, says things she later wishes she hadn't—it starts to tamper with the senses, coordination, and balance.

A woman having at least two drinks a day is on her way to active alcoholism. In the middle stages of alcoholism, she starts looking forward to her first drink early in the day and has one by lunchtime or sooner. She's now beginning to have a harder time getting an effect from each drink. Myra tells her story:

"I was drinking at least four drinks a night to survive my loneliness after my son left for college and my husband died. Suddenly I began to lose weight for no reason. When tests diagnosed colon cancer, I checked into a hospital, where I was unable to drink for two weeks. After the initial withdrawal was over, it was an uplifting experience for me, an unexpected chance to take a look at myself and my unhealthy habits. Doctors there recommended that I join Alcoholics Anonymous, which I did. Though I had several more bouts with alcohol, precipitated mainly by loneliness problems, I ended up free of it. I don't drink at all today. I'm not even tempted when I am alone, although I am often still very lonely."

Alcohol is ultimately a fatal fix, but not in the way you might expect. It is true that if you drink enough alcohol it affects the vital life centers by totally relaxing the muscles that control breathing. But a drinker rarely gets that far without vomiting or going into a coma first, which prevents her from taking the fatal drink. If heavy drinking goes on for years, however, the liver becomes inefficient or blocked (cirrhosis). The drinker has an increased risk of mouth, esophagus, stomach, and breast cancers. Alcohol may also affect the nervous system, triggering amnesia, disorientation, loss of short-term memory, hallucinations, emotional disturbances, loss of muscle control, double vision, and, possibly, depression, aggression, antisocial behavior, and anxiety—exactly the states of mind the woman wanted to escape when she began drinking. And to think that alcohol is available without prescription. Not even her doctor needs to know.

Beyond these side effects on herself are the recently identified side effects on an unborn baby. These effects are called Fetal Alcohol Syndrome (FAS): the baby is smaller, may have deformities of the limbs, joints, and fingers, and heart defects. Six or more drinks a day are enough to produce FAS. Even one binge in the first three months of pregnancy, including the first few weeks before the woman knows she's pregnant, may do it. Almost all obstetricians and gynecologists advise women who are pregnant or might be to avoid alcohol.

Staff members at the Betty Ford Center in Rancho Mirage, California, claim that the two obstacles their alcoholic clients have the hardest time overcoming are denial and admitting that they need help from someone outside themselves. The two aren't so different from each other. When a woman admits to alcoholism, she is admitting that she has lost the control over the life that she was trying to bolster by drinking. No one, male or female, wants to hit rock bottom that way. Denial is perhaps the most frustrating part of alcoholism. The alcoholic's family has given up on her, she's lost her job, her health is failing, and perhaps she's in debt. Still she blames everything but the alcohol for the mess she's in. Alcohol is still for her a way of dealing with it all.

Society is particularly unkind to the woman alcoholic. She receives far less sympathy and far more scorn than a man would. Although a woman today may have *all* the stresses of a man's life—workplace pressures, financial pressures, a family to support—plus others all her own, such as her monthly cycles and their attendant ups and downs, pregnancy, menopause, growing old in a youth culture, sex-role conflicts, the nursing of family members, and chauvinism, she is not expected to grab a beer at the end of the day to relax.

If you suspect you're a compulsive drinker but aren't sure, ask yourself these questions:

Do you often drink more than you intended?	yes	no
Have you ever promised yourself you will cut down on drinking but failed?	yes	no
Do you plan your activities around being able to drink?	yes	no
Do you drink when you're depressed or angry?	yes	no
Do you make excuses for your drinking?	yes	no
Have you developed friendships with others because they drink?	yes	no

Do you drink before going to a party when you know alcohol will be available there?	yes	no
Do you drink to relax or fall asleep?	yes	no
Do you eat very little or inconsistently when you're drinking?	yes	no
Do you sometimes get the "shakes" in the morning?	yes	no
Do you sometimes have memory blackouts and can't remember what you said while drinking?	yes	no
Do you come from a family with an alcoholic parent?	yes	no

If you've said "yes" to even one of these questions, you need some help. If you've said "yes" to two or more, you need help right now. You are abusing alcohol and cannot afford to wait before you admit it and get help.

Sometimes an alcoholic doesn't know exactly what it was that triggered her return to sobriety. Maybe it's simply that she reached her capacity for the pain of alcohol abuse or the pain it causes others. Sometimes she is frightened by the physical damage the drug has caused her. No matter at what stage an alcoholic really decides to take back control of her life, therapists agree that she can recover if she's determined to.

If you think you are an alcoholic, find out all you can about women alcoholics from local alcohol groups or the library. Jane, who was once an alcoholic, says she first got the push she needed to recover after she read two books: *Women Under the Influence: Alcohol and Its Impact* by Brigid McConville (Schocken Books, 1985), and *Goodbye Hangovers, Hello Life: Self-Help for Women* by Jean Kirkpatrick (Atheneum, 1986).

There are plenty of organizations to help—look under "Alcoholism" in the Yellow Pages and in the back of this book for information about other organizations. Sources include hospitals, private clinics, alcoholism counselors, psychologists, psychiatrists and psychiatric social workers. Many are inexpensive and confidential. Most groups or one-on-one counselors help the recovering alcoholic build a bridge back to real life by focusing on peer interaction and learning to identify and express feelings. Women today have the choice of a handful of programs designed especially for them. Some now provide child care, the absence of which has stood in the way of treatment for millions of woman-years.

Marijuana and Higher: The Grass Seems Greener

Turning on with psychedelic drugs may have become most widespread in the 1960s, but it is not gone in the eighties. Many women started to use this fix then; many have found it more recently. For some women, marijuana or "grass" makes happiness seem to be in their own backyard. For a few hours, they're euphoric, sensual, sociable, and likely to find the universe fascinating and their companions hilarious.

> "In college I majored in art, with a minor in pot smoking. There was lots of it around in those days. Other stuff, too. I still smoke every day, including on the job. I'm a mailman, or is it mailwoman? Anyway, I do all of my deliveries on foot, and smoking before I go out on my route makes it fun. Maybe it slows me down a little, but I really enjoy talking to the kids, petting the cats, and just looking around and feeling the sun. I smoke with my friends, too. We hang out, listen to music, eat ice cream, and laugh."

According to a survey published in *Ms.* Magazine (February 1987), 6.4 percent of *Ms.* readers turn regularly to psychoactive (mind-altering) drugs like marijuana and hashish. If that percentage applied to all the women in the United States, it could translate into thousands of women.

In the same survey, nearly three quarters of the respondents disagreed with the statement, "When I am not involved in a steady romantic sexual relationship, I feel less worthwhile as a person," so drugs aren't a major consolation for the manless woman. Why then do women turn to psychoactive or psychedelic (mind-expanding) drugs? To laugh, to relax, to escape, and especially to feel, since these drugs affect the five senses. Food is more inviting; touch is more sensual; aromas, music, and sights are more riveting. With increased dosages of psychedelic drugs, sensory crossovers can create stunning hallucinogenic effects: music has colors, inanimate objects breathe. Psychoactive and psychedelic drugs are letting-it-out fixes because they relieve the user of control.

These short-term physical side effects of occasional marijuana use are relatively minor: increased heart rate, sleepiness, altered depth perception, muscular weakness, trouble moving and reacting. With LSD and related drugs such as peyote and mescaline, the pupils of the eyes dilate, but other effects vary widely, depending upon what kind of psychological changes are happening.

Heavy drug use is no free trip: long-term smoking of marijuana contributes to memory impairment, lung inflammation, and possibly lung cancer. A pregnant woman who smokes marijuana is more likely than a non-smoking pregnant woman to have a spontaneous abortion, stillbirth, or smaller-than-normal baby. And someone who spends an afternoon tripping on acid (LSD) can have a surprise "flashback" of visual or sensory disturbances more than a year later.

The bad trip is another risk, both physically and psychologically.

"One night I was at home alone and decided to smoke a joint and watch MTV. Maybe the pot was stronger than usual or the mood I was in had something to do with it. I was watching a special on the Rolling Stones and began hearing things in the words and music that I had never heard before. Mick Jagger had always been sort of a turn-on for me, but that night I looked at him and the group and thought, *These guys are incredibly, incredibly evil.* I got frightened and began to feel cold, and I had this sense of the night being very evil and dark. So I closed all the curtains, put on a flute concerto, took a hot bath, and got into bed with some hot cocoa and a cookie. I basically had to nurse myself into a better mood. I think that if I had been less experienced with marijuana, it could have been a very bad evening."

Suggestibility, anxiety, confusion, restlessness, decreased concentration, distortion of the senses, difficulty in communicating—these commonplace side effects can be tragic. What if the user believes she can fly out a fifth-floor window? Or becomes so confused she thinks the surface of a lake is a paved parking lot? Or is unable to communicate pain? Drugs can deepen a depression, stir up low-grade anger, release tears and fears, or bring on an attack of paranoia.

Although psychoactive and psychedelic drugs aren't addictive, reverse-tolerance can develop. A woman can find herself needing *less* of her drug of choice to get high. Soon she will be leaving reality more rapidly behind. If reality is troublesome, the escape is enticing but temporary—the troubles will still be there when she comes down, making drugs a small, temporary comfort.

It may be a simple issue of control that leads a woman to interrupt a drug habit.

Marsha, an accountant, used marijuana every day. Although she never admitted it to herself, she was rarely straight. She'd sneak off into the ladies' room to smoke, and she'd smoke in her car, often while on the lookout for the police. At home, she'd light up every night. Since her boyfriend smoked and her close friends tolerated her behavior, it rarely got in the way.

One day, Marsha found her supply was out. None of her friends was around to give her any. She realized it would be two days before she could stock up again, and she panicked. "I called in sick to work for the next two days," she recalls, "and I spent terrible hours alone in my apartment, going crazy, thinking about how much I wanted to smoke. It was then that I recognized I had no control. I wanted to break free so I could make the choice of how to spend my time, and not allow anything else to determine my lifestyle. I joined a self-help group and began therapy, and now I'm happier. I have new friends who aren't heavy drug users. I still smoke occasionally, but it's recreational. I choose to get high instead of having to."

Marsha's decision was based on her feeling that she needed to control the choices in her life. Your reasons might be different, but they should focus on your own importance. How effective can a treatment program be if you feel you're unworthy or unlovable? The best drug programs today get the drugs out of your system *and* help you figure out what it was about life that made you want to alter it in the first place.

Your ultimate goal is to get control over your life. And make it better.

Tranquilizers and Sleeping Pills: The "Just-in-Case" Fixes

Every woman has to live through a crisis at some time in her life. Husbands are assigned to a new office across the country, children get into trouble, parents fall ill and need care. Even a job promotion for the woman herself can be a crisis if it fills her with stress. At times like these a woman is likely to wonder if a tranquilizer would help her through, help her keep on being there for the ones who need her most.

The doctor who agrees that the woman is going through a short-term, high-anxiety reaction to a real-life crisis will probably prescribe a tranquilizer—Valium, Librium, and Xanax are among the most popular. These sedative-hypnotic drugs will quiet the buzz in her head, relax her body, and enable her to think clearly about the problems at hand, one at a time, without the drowsiness some over-the-counter calmers bring.

If she's unable to sleep, the doctor may prescribe short-term barbiturate treatment with Seconal, Nembutal, or Haldol. These sedative-hypnotics help toward a full night's sleep. So far, no problem. The quick fix does its job, the crisis ends, and the woman's life returns to its normal chaos.

It's what happens to the pills after the crisis is over that turns a quick fix into a fatal fix.

Valerie had married at nineteen against her parents' wishes. She felt she wouldn't find another man like Ron and didn't want to wait.

One night less than a year into the marriage, Ronnie arrived home from work to find Valerie not home—she was out shopping with a girlfriend. Even though she returned a few minutes later carrying a store shopping bag, Ronnie was very suspicious and accused her of having an affair with someone from her office that she'd barely noticed. After several more of these confrontations over the next month, Ronnie actually slapped Valerie, shoved her, and called her a liar. Valerie had no experience with physical violence— she had come from a quiet home—and she felt that given the situation, she couldn't ask her parents for advice. So she turned to a well-meaning friend, who provided her with some leftover Librium. Valerie found that slipping away to take a pill made it easier for her to smile at Ronnie through her terror when he came home in a bad mood.

Valerie had found a way to make a less-than-perfect world look rosy without any repainting. In time, she found that if she took a Librium around five o'clock, just before she left work, she could avoid the terror of her situation altogether.

Lynn arrived at a similar conclusion with Valium:

Lynn's older daughter was a week away from her wedding date when Lynn's pregnant younger girl was in a car accident, which was not serious, but the doctors did want her to stay in the hospital for a few days for observation and feet-up rest. Though Lynn had already had wedding management experience, this was too much. She headed straight for the family practitioner. He prescribed Valium to help her get through the millions of small details she had to attend to. The Valium worked like magic, and Lynn was surprised that she felt fairly happy as she checked all the final wedding arrangements and monitored her younger daughter's progress between tasks.

After the wedding, Lynn slid into a major post-wedding

letdown. She began to think about the Valium that were still in the vial: Would they help her feel more like cleaning up the final corners of party mess and cooking a nice dinner for her husband? They did. Her doctor continued to renew her prescription, very few questions asked.

Within a year, Lynn had evolved a new attitude toward her Valium: Why not take some Valium ahead of time and *prevent* those "down" moments? Before a visit with a tiresome, talkative relative, before a tension-filled speech to the League of Women Voters, before a long, boring afternoon alone—Lynn was beginning to think she never needed to feel any of life's lows again.

Lynn would have been wiser to take a look at her life to see what it was about it that was making her so low. Chances are good that she was medicating "empty-nest" sensations: Her children were both married now, leaving her to do . . . what? She needed to rethink her personal goals. Had Lynn recognized that she was just going through a normal transition, she might never have been tempted to reach for the extra Valium. By taking them preventively, she prevented herself from working through some very legitimate feelings.

Women have taught themselves how to use the barbiturates as preventive medicine, too.

Like her father, Janeen is a brilliant scientist. Also like her father, Janeen has always been "high-strung": she reacts with great offense to well-meaning comments, is dogged in her pursuit of the truth no matter how it might hurt other people, and has trouble sleeping a couple of nights a week. She feels so dragged out the next morning that it's hard for her to look forward to her day, knowing she looks lousy and is likely to make errors in the lab.

Janeen believed that lying awake alone worrying about

the future of the world, the sad state of basic research, and her own future was her lot in life until she mentioned her insomnia to a doctor. He suggested she try some over-the-counter medications occasionally. When they failed, he prescribed a barbiturate, Seconal. What a relief! Not only did she sleep deeply and dreamlessly, but she awoke refreshed, almost cheerful, and feeling very competent to do her work.

Janeen began to use Seconals *in case* she was in for a rough night, and soon she had to take two to get to sleep, then three, then four. Recently, her insomnia has come back, and she is more crotchety during the day than she has ever been before. Co-workers in the lab have commented on it, and even her father, the one person who has always understood her, can't stand to be near her.

Sleeping pill addiction and withdrawal presents much higher health risks for women than lack of sleep. Too many women, fearing that fatigue will interfere with their ability to function like Superwoman, worry excessively about their ability to get a good night's sleep. Their anxiety leads them to take barbiturates or sedatives or psychedelics or alcohol even before they test their ability to fall asleep that night. They are medicating themselves "just in case." Others worry so much that they indeed can't fall asleep easily. They then reach for a pill.

A woman who has persistent difficulty with falling asleep or early waking may need psychological evaluation. Lying awake at night worrying about illness, the future, safety, social life, about absent children, about growing older, or about a sleeping mate who is so close and yet so far away can be a sign of an anxiety disorder or depression. Medication may be covering up such anxieties or depression—and isn't helping. Remember, however, that the older we get, the less sleep we need. In fact, most of us need less sleep than we think. A woman over fifty may be able to do well on five hours. So if you are sleeping less but waking up refreshed and falling asleep easily, don't reach for pills!

Sedative-hypnotics are a strong alternative to dealing with real-life problems, and they create a physical dependency with regular use. In small doses, they bring relaxation and mild euphoria. In larger doses—which the regular user eventually needs—the effects can be slurred speech, slowed reflexes, trouble walking, mental confusion, drowsiness, or, if the dose is high enough, unconsciousness or death, as the drugs relax the muscles that control circulation and breathing to the point that they stop working altogether. Death can also come from overdose: in your grogginess, it's easy to forget how many pills you've taken and retake a dose "just to be sure." The barbiturate addict who survives for the long term may find herself experiencing highly unwelcome anxiety, insomnia, paranoia, and suicidal depression.

Barbiturates and tranquilizers, like alcohol, depress the central nervous system. Like alcohol, barbiturates, and some benzodiazepines (especially Valium—the one the Rolling Stones called "Mother's little helper") are addictive. Tolerance develops and a woman needs a larger and larger dose of her liquid barbiturate (alcohol) or her pills to get the same effect she used to get on less medication. The user who misses her fix may get the shakes, also known as delirium tremens or DTs; have a rapid pulse; feel weak, anxious, and restless; or hallucinate. She may even go into life-threatening convulsions or exhaustion due to a temporary psychosis. When these medications are used as secret sleep fixes, further danger is introduced since an overdose or withdrawal symptoms will not be identified easily and can be misdiagnosed. It's absolutely essential to have a doctor's help when you decide you're ready to shake off a sedative-hypnotic addiction. If you suspect you're over-using benzodiazepines or barbiturates, don't hide it. If Betty Ford can tell all, you certainly can.

Stimulants: Too Much of a Good Thing

Most women suspect themselves of being stimulus junkies—the more we give ourselves to do, the more we get done. We'd rather push ourselves and feel the fatigue of accomplishment than take it easy and feel the guilt of an unfinished list. We allow those little demons, the "shoulds," to run our lives: I *should* make the chocolate mousse from scratch, I *should* sew Jennifer a costume for the school play, I *should* spend an evening at the college fund-raiser phoneathon. We overplan our Sundays, the traditional day of rest, and we need at least a two-day vacation transition period to slow down enough to relax on a beach.

Stimulation is good in some ways. Many women are actually happier and healthier when they're on the move. There is a distinction, though, between stimulation and stress. They both keep a woman running, but the difference is all-important. I call a demand that you've chosen stimulation; moving to your dream house, becoming a corporate officer after working for the promotion, playing a competitive game of tennis, running for political office, or organizing a tenants' committee. Stress, on the other hand, is a demand that is thrust upon you, over which you have no control: nursing an ill or dying parent, job hunting after being fired, adjusting to widowhood, moving away from friends and family because your husband has been transferred, or experiencing an early menopause when you were planning to have another child.

The typical stimulus junkie starts her day with a long list of self-assigned chores, errands, projects, favors, business meetings, repair appointments, shopping trips, deliveries, carpool pickups and dropoffs, office orders, telephone calls. To this list of selected activities, life often adds the unexpected demands that I call stress: a visit with her son's teacher, a run to the hospital when a friend has emergency surgery, a stop at the bank to cover a check, a trip to the hardware store to buy a new sump pump, or a quarter of an hour on the telephone trying to convince the plumber he has to come today. Unfortunately, the typical stimulus junkie doesn't eliminate the optional items on her list to make room for the unexpected ones. Soon she's on overload, with too much to do and too little time to do it in. The adrenaline pours out, the blood sugar burns up, and she burns out. The quick fix? A stimulant.

Which stimulants do women choose? Caffeine, nicotine, amphetamines, or even cocaine. The feeling is familiar. With both real-life stimulants and artificial ones, our heart pumps more quickly, our respiration is increased, our mind seems sharper, our appetite is temporarily suppressed. Depression is counteracted, delayed, or disguised temporarily. For the moment there's no need to feel we're losing life's battle by slowing down or running out of steam. Adeptly handling the stimulations and stresses life dishes out reinforces our feeling of importance, usefulness, and competence. With an artificial stimulant to help, we feel very much alive and ready for anything!

All of the artificial stimulants share some effects on the central nervous system, which includes the brain and the spinal cord. In general, they kick us into action and reduce inhibitions by:

- stimulating the cerebral cortex, which handles thought processes, and other parts of the brain which are the centers of energy, action, and optimism;
- stimulating the medulla, which regulates heart rate, respiration, and coordination;

o signaling the release of adrenaline, which stimulates the nerve cells that trigger our action muscles.

Caffeine, nicotine, amphetamines, and cocaine all offer a fast fix for the woman who thinks she must keep going and going. Long term, these fixes can be fatal to her mind, her body, and her quality of life.

Caffeine: The Domesticated Upper

We live in a caffeine culture: you can buy a coffee machine that turns itself on in the morning before you wake up, filling the house with a "heavenly aroma." If you have an office job, the cart comes around at ten and three, or there's a free supply at the coffee machine. If you work at home, it's friendly to take a tea or coffee break with a neighbor. In the city, it's fashionable to have tea in the afternoon in one of the large hotels. Caffeine is the domesticated stimulant the busy woman can always count on.

Caffeine is one of a group of rejuvenating chemical compounds called *xanthines*. It stimulates the central nervous system, boosting metabolism, increasing cardiac activity, and releasing sugar into the bloodstream. The effects on you are energy, alertness, and greater endurance for an hour or two. Caffeine boosts simple motor activity, giving you get-up-and-go for chores and routines (not for complex activities like repairs or calligraphy, though). Caffeine also arouses your sensory neurons, making dessert or a cigarette more flavorful. If you take another drug, like aspirin, you may find it more potent. Finally, caffeine is a mild diuretic.

But a dangerous drug? In some cases, yes—absolutely.

Nancy was the mother of a three-month-old baby and a two-year-old, a first-time homeowner, the newest member of the local church, *and* a writer who wanted to keep her contacts current. Though all the child-care books advised her to take a nap when her baby slept, she felt she needed the time to write. After the sitter had shepherded the toddler off to the playground, Nancy would immediately brew up a cup of strong coffee and take it with her to the computer, where she would type like a demon until either the baby woke up or the sitter came back.

When the baby was four months old, Nancy added an after-dinner espresso—it helped her do church work or a little more writing after the children were in bed.

Now that the baby is walking, Nancy is drinking two cups of coffee with breakfast to wake up, a cup around ten so she can keep on unpacking those never-ending boxes from the move, two more cups at lunch, a cup to write by, and the espresso. Funny, though—the effect isn't what it used to be. Plus, she's having stomach trouble, her heart pounds for no reason, and she finds herself sitting bolt upright in bed around 1:00 A.M. every night.

As you've probably guessed, Nancy is drinking too much coffee. She's getting so much caffeine, in fact—the equivalent of seven to ten cups of coffee a day—that her tolerance has increased so that she isn't getting the same boost out of it. If she doesn't cut back, two other symptoms of caffeinism, delirium and sensory disturbances, may disrupt her routine even more.

The first thing a woman who drinks this much coffee or its caffeine equivalent needs to do is to take her addiction seriously! Coffee is indeed an addiction, just like alcohol, tranquilizers, and barbiturates, which means that cutting back is a real physical challenge. A coffee lover who stops drinking coffee is likely to go through withdrawal symptoms every bit as unpleasant as the side effects of too much caffeine: irritability, lethargy, and headaches. A good way to begin is to make coffee or tea gradually less and less strong, dilute it with milk, and drink only after meals, when it will cause less gastrointestinal irritation.

Nicotine: Fast Fix, Slow Death

It is fascinating and horrifying that smoking is becoming such a major addiction for women. Why should a smelly, messy, traditionally male habit like smoking attract women? Perhaps for exactly that reason: Smoking makes a statement that "I am tough" in a time when some women may still be a bit uncomfortable in the working world. For both sexes, sitting down with a cigarette is a time out, instant springtime, a pause that refreshes; for the busy woman who feels unentitled to any time for herself, it's a valuable and approved break. According to a recent survey, women who work outside the home and women who are separated or divorced are more likely to smoke than housewives.

Since most smokers begin smoking as teenagers, there are also elements of peer pressure and of defiance—*Who is the Surgeon General to tell me what to do? What do my parents know about me and my life?* Although the number of smokers is dropping for both males and females, the females have been slower as a group. More than 26 million adult American women smoke, including about a quarter of all pregnant women.

Besides giving a harried woman the chance to sit down for a moment, a smoke carries a potent chemical, nicotine, to the brain within seconds of the first inhale. There, it lifts mood, reduces appetite (an effect sanctioned by a figure-obsessed society), and temporarily fights fatigue. A lifetime of cigarette smoking has other effects you've probably already heard about:

186

cancers of the mouth, throat, larynx, esophagus, lungs, bladder, kidney, and pancreas; lung disease, heart disease; and aggravation of peptic ulcers, high blood pressure, and sleep disorders. A woman smoker who uses oral contraceptives has a much higher chance of cardiovascular problems than the woman who doesn't smoke. Smoking contributes to Buerger's disease, in which the blood vessels constrict and can cause gangrene. In pregnant women, the nicotine and other chemicals circulate through the fetus's body, later contributing to fetal problems such as low birth weight, short stature in the child, and impaired reading ability. Pregnant smokers also have a higher risk of spontaneous abortion and stillbirth.

Since this fast fix may not become a fatal fix for a long time, smokers often feel no urgency about quitting. Their reasoning is that the small comfort and immediate benefits, which include avoiding the withdrawal symptoms, are worth it. Well, they're not worth it.

> Gloria had begun smoking when she was eighteen and starting her first job as a typist. Everyone else in the typing pool smoked except one prim girl, and Gloria didn't want to be classed with her. By age twenty-five, Gloria decided she might be more attractive to men if she quit—her breath, clothes, and hair would be fresher, and she wouldn't cough so much in the morning. She managed to stop smoking just long enough to get married. At work, however, she was told to take a course in word processing, and the stress was enough to reawaken her cigarette habit. She used the pauses in her smoking ritual to collect herself, sit back, and process all the new information she was expected to take in. At home, smoking was a way to sit on the couch for a moment, an immunity from the demands of her husband and little girl.
>
> By age thirty-five, Gloria's cough worsened and she

187

began to have real trouble breathing. The eventual diagnosis: emphysema, a respiratory disease in which the lungs lose their elasticity and it becomes impossible to exhale stale air fully. Though medication controlled her emphysema most of the time, the disease progressed, and Gloria found herself hospitalized three times in the next five years. Amazingly, she continued to smoke, going so far as to beg hospital visitors for cigarettes. Gloria died at forty-one.

I include this sad story for a reason. It's often very difficult for anybody to envision the future consequences of today's actions, but for smokers, doing so can be a lifesaver. The anecdote also illustrates just how powerful nicotine's hold can be. I've heard of hospital patients trying to smoke in oxygen tents after lung surgery!

A smoker who decides to quit will have the best chance if she quits on her own. Of the 2 million Americans who quit smoking each year, 95 percent do it without outside help. This means that the woman who feels too busy to sign up for another class or course has just lost that excuse. Whether you quit cold turkey or bit by bit is up to you: "habit" smokers can go either way, but for "addicted" smokers it's all or nothing.

To Nix the Cigarette Fix

The following—plus your own willpower—may help you to quit smoking:

- List your reasons for quitting: your kids, your breath, the way the house smells, the cost of your habit.
- Emphasize the immediate benefits: more stamina, no more hacking cough, no more cigarette burns in your clothing, a cleaner house.

- Study your smoking habit. Under what circumstances are you likely to smoke: when you're drinking? driving? on the phone? with certain friends? Avoid those situations if you can.
- Plan your quitting several weeks in advance. Learn what to expect: withdrawal symptoms include nervousness, drowsiness, depression, anxiety, lightheadedness, nausea, headaches, constipation or diarrhea, sweating and, most of all, cravings! Prepare to replace smoking with brisk walks, yoga, sculpture, worry beads—anything to distract your mind and hands.
- Enlist the help of friends and family.
- Get rid of all cigarettes and smoking paraphernalia.
- Examine your diet. Food will begin to taste good again, so keep a supply of carrot sticks, chewing gum, and other low-calorie snacks on hand. This is not, however, the time to go on a strict diet—too much too soon.
- Get more exercise.
- Spend as much time as you can in places where no smoking is allowed. Go to the library or a museum. Sit in the non-smoking section of the movie house. In some states, going to work means "no smoking allowed," too!
- Reward yourself. Save your cigarette money for a trip or a CD player. Or buy yourself flowers, easy paperbacks, fragrant soap, a magazine subscription.

If all else fails, a medical doctor may be able to prescribe drugs that will help you stop smoking. *Clonidine,* used to treat opiate withdrawal; *naltrexone,* for heroin addiction; and *mecamylamine,* for hypertension, are all in the experimental stages with regard to nicotine withdrawal. Nicotine gums and sprays may help a *habit* smoker break the smoking cycle, but they do not break the nicotine addiction.

Amphetamines: Passing the Speed Limit

Another name for one class of amphetamines is "speed," and that sums it up. On amphetamines, you practically fly. These stimulants produce intense alertness and false confidence. A woman on amphetamines, who only just a few minutes before was too tired to decide what video to have delivered, is now ready to send out a few résumés and then make some calls to find a date before the movie she wants to see begins. Amphetamine users become talkative, excited, and restless, and feel endlessly energetic and boundlessly insightful. The huge energy rush makes amphetamines especially popular with students, performers, athletes, and truck drivers, among others.

> Eileen was going to be a lawyer no matter how many obstacles they threw at her. Her husband was still giving her a hard time about moving nearer to the law school where she'd been accepted. He hadn't let one chance go by to remind her that his pay cut was because of her. And though he had shown some sympathy for her huge workload, he still somehow expected a good dinner and good sex. Often after he went to sleep, Eileen would get up, get dressed, take a "pep pill," and go back to school to work in the law journal office or in the library, where she did some low-paying research for her property professor. Before a moot court session in which the judge was a professor known to be rough on female students, Eileen took two pills. They made her feel sharper and more able to parry with him.

Eileen did not end up addicted to amphetamines but she did become psychologically dependent during law school and experienced many of the side effects of amphetamines: decreased appetite, weight loss, a dry mouth and nose, a higher body temperature, a more rapid heartbeat, higher blood pressure, and faster breathing. Once she had her diploma and a job in a large, civilized firm where junior associates were not abused, she was able to stop taking the pills and gain back the weight she'd lost.

Other women aren't quite so lucky. The working mother who uses amphetamines to navigate a nineteen-hour day, the advertising executive who depends on them to get her through a busy period that never ends, the shy woman who gets hooked on the volubility amphetamines bring her—these women are in trouble. A regular user may find that one pill doesn't do what it used to do, but too many cause an irregular heartbeat, restlessness, dizziness, anxiety, and aggressive and violent behavior. With regular use, amphetamines may bring fatigue, a loss of appetite that results in malnutrition, depression or suicidal thoughts, and even paranoia and other psychoses or breaks with reality.

Getting off amphetamines is as difficult as kicking a caffeine or cigarette habit. A user who stops using will "crash" and feel tired, depressed, and anxious. Once she succeeds, she needs to take a look at the reasons she started taking amphetamines in the first place. Was it boredom? Fatigue? Depression? Are those reasons still there, ready to push her toward some other addiction with its attending complications? A woman with a willing attitude—or a friend who is willing to take her hand and lead her to a therapist—is the one who will shake the "speed-freak" label for good. Medical and psychological support can increase her chances of staying speed-free.

Cocaine Kicks Back

Fortunately, cocaine is no longer the status drug it once was. Enough celebrities and prominent people have paid for its effects with their careers or lives to make even the thought of snorting it through a hundred-dollar bill seem unglamorous now. Rock stars and athletes have come out publicly against drugs of all kinds. Still, the national cocaine hotline takes about one thousand calls a day, nearly half of which are from women. What the celebrities know, the rest of us are just beginning to find out.

It's estimated that 20 percent of the women who use cocaine are dependent. Why? Most doctors agree that it's a combination of factors that allow women to become dependent on any drug. Chief among them are stress and anxiety, the result of having to be mother, career woman (and often chief breadwinner), homemaker, lover, and beauty simultaneously.

Cocaine and its cousin, crack, are also stimulants and act on the central nervous system, raising the breathing rate, heart rate, blood pressure, and body temperature. Like all the other stimulants, they wake you up and shut your appetite down. At the peak of the high, which comes on quickly because cocaine is absorbed through the nasal mucous membranes, a user feels an all-surpassing well-being and warmth toward other people and a sense of great personal power and intelligence. Since women have a significantly higher incidence of depression and often a higher fear of failure than men, cocaine can be a particularly seductive drug for them. Cocaine also numbs pain, including hunger pangs. All of these effects account for the immense popularity of Coca-Cola in the 1800s—it contained a small amount of cocaine! In 1909, the U.S. Food and Drug

Administration brought action against Coca-Cola, and that was the end of cocaine-in-a-bottle. Now caffeine is the stimulant in most sodas. Cocaine was also the main ingredient in most of the invigorating tonics and miracle elixirs of the last century.

Like amphetamines, cocaine can cause a psychological dependence, since users often find it hard to get along without its pleasant high.

Kelly came from Oklahoma to New York hoping to get modeling jobs. She had just the kind of intelligent face and curvy body the magazines were looking for. Once she registered with a model agency, things began to happen quickly. She was hired for several $150-an-hour jobs in her first week of work and by Friday night was at a loft party on the arm of a photographer, mingling with other photographers, other models, hairstylists, art directors. Though her boss at the agency had reminded her that drinking would leave her with tiny broken blood vessels in her nose and around the eyes, she had said nothing about cocaine, so when her date offered her some, she took it. And liked it: It made her feel as if she belonged in this sophisticated crowd. The feeling was worth the slight depression that followed after the cocaine wore off. Nor did she mind the loss of appetite—after all, she was a model.

Soon Kelly learned that cocaine was offered occasionally at photo shoots, and she always accepted. It seemed to dissolve her fears of not being good enough and made it easier to shift smoothly from one photogenic expression to the next. Lately, however, Kelly has been finding the lights very bright and the sessions too long. Everybody wants poses; nobody is interested in *her* expressions. She talks back to her boss and sasses photographers. Although the number of male photographers willing to keep her supplied

193

with cocaine hasn't changed, the number of modeling calls for her has tapered off, and she's beginning to believe that she's been blacklisted by the industry.

Kelly is in the grips of two of the common long-term effects of regular cocaine use: restlessness and paranoia. Kelly hasn't exactly been blacklisted, but her behavior has made her unpleasant to work with and she is definitely unpopular. She is lucky to have escaped some of the other long-term effects of cocaine. Her career might have ended much sooner if she were experiencing sleeplessness and hallucinations, one of which, *formication*, is particularly unpleasant. When experiencing formication, the cocaine user has the sensation that insects or snakes are crawling under the skin. A chronic user can also damage the mucous membranes inside of her nose. We know now too, after the heart attack deaths of at least one healthy young athlete, that taking cocaine is playing cardiac roulette. An old Cole Porter song goes, "Some get a kick from cocaine." How many users of cocaine must have wished they weren't among them!

Kicking Cocaine

Recognizing your addiction is the first step toward a drug-free life. If *any* of these statements applies to you, your quick fix needs attention now.

1. I'm using a drug or drugs frequently in order to get high.
2. I say I can stop any time, but I haven't done it.
3. I make sure I always have a supply of the drug on hand.
4. I sometimes lie to my friends about what I'm doing.
5. I feel guilty about my drug use.

6. At least one person in my family also uses drugs frequently.
7. I hang out with people who also use the drug or drugs I use.
8. I sometimes miss work or family functions because of my drug use.
9. I have developed a tolerance to the drug and use it more often or in higher dosages as a result.
10. I am spending too much money on my drug.
11. I have physically endangered myself or others while high on the drug.
12. I sneak away at work or at home to take the drug privately.

Researchers are beginning to believe that cocaine may be somewhat physically addicting. Kicking a cocaine habit takes serious psychological counseling, plenty of support, and solid medical backup. A good place to start is the national cocaine hotline number, 1-800-COCAINE. If the line is busy, keep trying until you get through. The person on the other end will have lists of treatment centers near you.

More important, though, try to find out why you feel you need drugs—any kind. Are you escaping from loneliness, boredom, anger, stress? If so, ask yourself how you can deal with those feelings in a more constructive way.

If you can't quit cold turkey, make a deal with yourself to cut down. You may find that it's possible to go drug-free one or two days a week, then three or four. Keep increasing your days "off" until you no longer need the drug. Reward yourself with new hobbies, a book you've always wanted to read, or a trip you've always wanted to take. You've earned it and may now have the extra money.

Fill your free time with substitute activities that you enjoy, preferably in public places.

If you're seriously addicted to a hard-core drug, get medical help immediately. Your doctor may be able to help you find a program that will suit your needs. Don't think of asking for help as a sign of weakness. It's a sign of intelligence.

The fatal fixes are among the most difficult fixes to get control of. It makes sense. Everybody would kick her fatal fix if it were easy! If you are in a love/hate relationship with a fatal fix now, the smartest thing you can do is to turn your problem over to someone else. Someone who will not give up until you are free of your fatal fix for good.

NINE

Real Fixes

This chapter is for you and only you. No more stories about other people and their problems. You have a fix that needs fixing. Your fix has let you down, left you feeling guilty, or become more of a bother than the original bother.

Though you may feel helpless and passive about your fix, you chose your fix—it didn't choose you. You chose it because it made you feel better. Ask yourself:

If you chose shopping, are you feeling lonely? bored? low in self-esteem? ignored? unhappily married?

If you chose eating, are you tired? bored? sexually frustrated?

If you chose sleeping, are you feeling conflicted? sad? guilty? angry? overwhelmed? unhappy in bed?

If you chose sleeping pills, are you anxious? nervous? overwhelmed?

If you chose telephoning, are you feeling guilty? alone? afraid?

If you chose alcohol, are you inhibited? having nightmares? having daymares?

If you chose a mood-elevating drug, are you feeling depressed? anxious? unsexy? adrift?

If you chose a mind-altering drug, are you bored? tense? too much in control?

If you chose a stimulant like coffee, tea, amphetamines, or cocaine, are you overwhelmed? exhausted?

If you chose gambling, are you feeling bored? bereft? powerless? pessimistic? poor?

If you chose yelling, are you feeling insulted? boxed in? very, very angry about something else? Is hot weather getting on your nerves? Are you tired? Are you in the PMS stage of your monthly cycle when you yell?

If you chose dieting or cosmetics, are you feeling disheveled *inside?* unhappy about being you?

If you chose a big fix like a new house or a new baby, are you looking for more continuity in your life? more stability? more "cement"?

If you chose television, are you lonely? bored? not busy enough? too busy?

If you chose workaholism, are you unhappy at home? too tense not to work? in need of control or closure?

If you chose smoking (so long ago!), do you feel uncomfortable? different from the rest of the crowd? out of energy?

If you move furniture, do you really want to redecorate your life?

If you try to keep your house perfectly clean, do you secretly wish you *yourself* were perfect?

Your "yes" answers to the questions above give you a profile of your fix patterns—what you reach for when you don't take the time to reach out to yourself, and why you probably turned to those fixes that are no longer doing the trick.

Time to Focus on Yourself

Self-worth, self-esteem, self-renewal—your fix almost certainly has something to do with one of them. If you're low on self-worth or desperately in need of recharging, why wouldn't you try to cure those unpleasant feelings? It's perfectly natural. In fact, you've probably chosen a very efficient way to put your problems in a box, tie it up, and toss it out.

The biggest real fix of all is cleaning up the life situation that led you to reach for your small comfort, fast fix, secret fix, big bix, or fatal fix in the first place. I don't have to tell you that this is a long-term project. How much time did it take you to admit that your fix was just a cover-up? Weeks, months, or years? Fixing the fix may take just as long. If you know what to expect, it will be much easier for you to start examining yourself and your life.

What to Expect When Fixing a Fix

1. Expect change. You're about to confront your own emotions. You may have revelations about your life, and you may well act on them. If you do, your life will certainly change, and you may affect other people, too, perhaps taking them by surprise.

2. Expect opposition. Remember, the original purpose of your fix was to make life easier. As you push your fix away, others may not cherish the new you—if, for example, the new you is trying to quit smoking and is grouchy and irritable. For those around you, life is suddenly harder, not easier. Once your fix is past tense,

others may be jealous of your new health, assertiveness, or productivity.

3. Expect to feel alone. If other people do choose to help you, you still can't count on twenty-four-hour-a-day support. At times it's just you and your fix. Joining a group especially designed to address your fix, if there is such a group, can bring some camaraderie and pleasantness to your project. If no group is available, look for one-on-one counseling.

4. Expect to be afraid. What will life be like without your fix? If you can't imagine it, then life-after-fix must seem like a big, empty place to you. It won't be. We wouldn't call a real fix a fix at all if good feelings weren't waiting at the end. If you were motivated enough to pick up this book and read this far, then you're motivated enough to build the kind of life you want for yourself. Libraries are loaded with reading material on compulsions and addictions, yours included—a big help if you need a better fix on your direction.

5. Expect the transition to take time. If your dream is to wake up tomorrow a new person, please erase it from your mind now. An unrealistic expectation like this can undermine your strength and determination.

6. Expect self-criticism. As you reassess your situation, you may wonder how you could have put up with "it" for so long, whatever "it" may be. Or you may wonder how you could ever have fallen for your fix.

7. Expect to miss your old fix. Some transitions are smooth, and some are like a rocky and vertical climb. For a while, you may feel you're neither here nor there. If your fix was an actual physical addiction, you will feel its absence acutely for a while.

Find Something Else to Do

As you separate yourself from your fix, harmless substitutes and distractions can help a lot. Women who responded to my survey suggest:

- **Physical exercise.** Movement burns up adrenaline and tension. Walking, jogging, biking, swimming, dancing, even karate will leave you feeling comfortably tired at first, then actually energized as you become practiced.
- **Manual labor.** It can be constructive, rhythmic, and satisfying. Not cleaning, for example, but building—and I mean building, not having something built! Hammering, sawing, lifting, hauling . . . Another good way to use up adrenaline as you make a desk or a hothouse, or assemble a platform bed.
- **Going for a walk** with a little boy or girl, with the dog, or with your own thoughts. Besides dissipating adrenaline, a walk will give you a chance to put your life in perspective.
- **Trying a new skill,** like making bread,which includes kneading for a full ten minutes with lots of pounding. Imagine the bread board is something in your life that you'd like to pound on! It's a healthy way to divert anger that has nowhere to go, and you get fresh bread into the bargain.
- **Sharing a project like quilting or doing needlepoint with a friend.** If your friend knows you well and is trustworthy, you've got a therapeutic session as an extra benefit.
- **Reading.** Choose a really relaxing novel set in a time and place you enjoy. The escape can give your body and mind a restful mini-vacation.
- **Pampering yourself.** Do your nails and admire them, or

play with your hairstyle. Don't make these cosmetic changes for vanity reasons or to please other people! Think of them as expressions of yourself. Have as much fun as you did when you finger-painted in kindergarten.

o **Cleaning out your wallet or making a list.** There is something *so satisfying* about organizing a small corner of your life when all around is chaos. And don't confine your list to Things to Do Today. Make a list of people and actions that bother you and then cross them off as you act to improve situations. At night when you wake up with your mind in ferment, write what's troubling you on a slip of paper. Then tell yourself to go to sleep—your worries are safe until morning. (Buy one of those sanity-saving pencil and pad sets that come with a little light attached.)

o **Watching cartoons, horror flicks, or romantic movies.** The television and movies are powerful media that can help you express emotions that don't come out easily. Do you need to laugh, scream, cry, or sigh? A carefully selected show can trigger a release.

o **Keeping a journal.** It will be therapeutic for you to organize your thoughts and get them down on paper and out of your head. It will be enlightening for you to reread the journal later on.

o **Doing volunteer work.** Whenever you feel you have no more inner resources, helping other people can make you see how much you have to give.

o **Listening to music, playing the piano, singing.** Did you know that music releases endorphins, the body's natural painkillers? Try humming a fast tune to energize yourself or a slow tune to relax yourself, resurrecting an old tune with happy memories or belting out "When Will I Be Loved?" or "I Am Woman," and see if you feel better.

o **Praying or meditating.** Sometimes turning your problems over to a higher power, through prayer, can bring you the peace you need. For others, focusing inward or outward through meditation techniques can bring some peace.

o **Raking leaves or potting plants.** Many people find that gardening replaces tensions with pleasure. Smelling the earth and grass can help you forget the odor of ink, plastic, and pollution.

o **Visiting a historic house or an old inn.** Imagine how many people walked the creaky wooden floorboards before you were even born! Think about how many others have sat in the chairs, eaten at the tables, studied the wallpaper, enjoyed the sun coming in the window. You're not the first person who's had the problems you're having.

These harmless and pleasurable activities may not melt your troubles like lemon drops, but they may do two other things: make you feel sunny for a while and distract you from a less healthy kind of fix.

The Final Fix

Are you ready now for the real thing? To fix your life to be the way you want it—without fixes—you'll need a good grip on these basics:

1. *Total* self-honesty. Nobody knows you better than you, right? Not quite. One of the hallmarks of out-of-control behaviors is denial. Even when your fix has taken over your life, it is simply not human nature to see it clearly. Fixes are always symptoms of a syndrome. Ask yourself why you need your fix. If you can't figure out why, you need outside help—a counselor, a psychologist, a therapist, someone else who can be 100 percent objective about you. You say you don't *want* an outsider to be

objective about you? Take it as a sign that you need help more than you think you do.

2. Setting realistic expectations for yourself. Nobody is perfect, and there's no reason for you to expect perfection of yourself. If other people want you to be perfect, take a look at where their expectations are coming from. Could it be that they're trying to distract you from their own imperfections? Do they have an unrealistic concept of what life is about? Don't give others too much power over you. It's intelligent to accept outside observations about ways you can improve yourself, but it's your personal pleasure to name your goals and work toward them. No matter what, perfection shouldn't be anywhere on your list!

3. Understanding your own faults. Confronting weaknesses with your eyes wide open is the quickest self-repair that psychologists know of. Yes, it's painful to realize that you make mistakes again and again. Yes, it's embarrassing, even if you're admitting your faults only to yourself. Look at self-improvement as a quiet hobby you pursue for your own enjoyment. Learn all you can about how your family, friends, schooling, and profession contributed to the person you are now. Take heart in the fact that when it comes to needing repair work, you've got plenty of company.

4. Treasuring your strengths and accomplishments. Do you find it unnatural to praise your own strong points? You need to learn how. Many women (and men too) who see only their weaknesses grew up in families where "Congratulations!" was seldom heard. And you can believe that out there in the real world, few people take much time to tell you you're doing a good job. So, if no one else will do it for you, do it for yourself!

5. Rewarding yourself for steps in the right direction.

There's no reason why you can't modify your own behavior. Here's an example:

> You enjoy your fix, but there are other things in life
> that you may enjoy just as much: a long-stemmed rose,
> being waited on in a restaurant, having someone wash
> your hair, walking on the shore, taking a long bath,
> sitting down in a chair outside *without* a book or proj-
> ect. Each morning, decide what reward you will give
> yourself that day. If you function without your fix, give
> yourself the reward. As your good feelings about your-
> self increase, you can give larger rewards less fre-
> quently. Soon, being fix-free will be its own reward.

6. Understanding how society may have shaped you as a
   woman. It almost certainly conflicts with some of the
   ways you feel inside. Wives and mothers over fifty, for
   example, who were already well versed in passive perfectionism by the time the women's movement came along,
   are especially likely to feel some discomfort—*if* they
   allow themselves to. I have met so many capable older
   women who have not even begun to recognize their own
   talents. Their husbands certainly haven't. Why should
   they, when it would disrupt family life and break the
   chain of command? The woman who does recognize her
   potential is caught in a bind: She knows her worth but
   may be afraid to take the first tentative steps to prove it.
   Even women who are sure of themselves may have to
   jump many high fences enclosing male territories. It's
   hard work. Younger women don't have it easier. With so
   many choices hard won over the past decade and a half,
   they are often opting for them all and finding themselves
   burned out.

Self-fulfilling Strategies

Finally, I *believe* you can trade in your small comfort, quick fix, secret fix, big fix, or fatal fix for a more centered way of living. Women in our society are so accustomed to hearing we'll fail that we often plan on it. And believing it can make it happen.

The next time someone aims discouraging words at you— or the next time you aim some at yourself—ask yourself if you deserve to be treated that way. I'll tell you the answer: No, you don't. You deserve to make mistakes, to feel emotions, to say "yes," to say "no." You're entitled to an inner life of your own —filled with large comforts and without fixes. And you can have it. And you can share it with those who love you.

APPENDIX A

The Psychotherapies: What Kind of Help Is Best?

With change, the first step is often the biggest one. Though it is no physical challenge to pick up the Yellow Pages and start looking for the right kind of help, it is a psychological giant leap. To get you started, here is a list of the different types of therapists and some organizations you can call or write to for general information.

Experts recommend that you talk to two or three therapists before you decide on one. Things to ask about: training, whether they treat your kind of problem, fees. And most important, make sure the communication is good! You will be spending your time, effort, and money on your therapy. You will have a fuller, more enjoyable experience if the person you choose is someone with whom you feel you can be open.

Psychiatrists are medical doctors (M.D.s) who specialize in mental disorders. Look for one who is certified by the American Board of Psychiatry and Neurology.

Psychologists hold doctoral degrees (Ph.D.s) and specialize in research, teaching, psychological testing. **Clinical psychologists** have taken clinical training during their graduate studies and, in most states, have had at least two years of supervised experience treating patients.

Social workers help people with everyday personal and family problems. **Clinical social workers** have completed two years of graduate study plus two years of supervised postgraduate work. A clinical social worker can qualify to practice psychotherapy in most states.

Counselors offer vocational, educational and other kinds of guidance. A counselor who has completed a two-year graduate-level program that includes supervised clinical work and has earned a master's degree may be qualified to do psychotherapy in some states.

Family therapists who have completed a curriculum of study set out by the American Association for Marriage and Family Therapy plus two years of supervised postgraduate experience treat family and marital problems.

Certified pastoral counselors are certified by the American Association of Pastoral Counselors to offer health counseling within a religious context.

Psychiatric nurses who have had graduate training plus specialized mental health training may treat some mental health problems.

If you are not sure whether the helping person you have chosen is certified, contact the American Psychiatric Association, the American Psychological Association, the National Association of Social Workers, or the American Association of Marriage and Family Therapists. These organizations have branches in nearly every state and are listed in most telephone directories (look under county or state names rather than "American" or "National").

For names of certified mental health counselors near you, write to the American Mental Health Counselors Association, 5999 Stevenson Avenue, Alexandria, VA 22304.

For certified pastoral counselors, write to the American Association of Pastoral Counselors, 9508A Lee Highway, Fairfax, VA 22031.

You can also try the National Mental Health Association, which has 650 local and state chapters. All make referrals. Also check community mental health agencies and family service agencies.

APPENDIX B

Where to Get Help

The fact that this appendix is long should prove to you that help is available —plenty of it—no matter what the nature of your fix. At each center or organization, you will find people who will not be surprised by your problem and who will know exactly how to handle it.

It's best to make an appointment with each organization before planning a visit. Many will send printed information.

Alcohol and Drug Dependency

Hazelden, Box 11, Center City, MN 55012. 1-(612)-257-4010 (out of state, 1-[800]-262-5010). Private, residential treatment program. Individual and group therapy. About half of the nearly 200 patients are women.

Betty Ford Center, 39000 Bob Hope Drive, Rancho Mirage, CA 92270. 1-(800)-392-7540 (out of state, 1-[800]-854-9211). Typical stay is twenty-eight days. Includes an outpatient program.

Women's Alcoholism Center, 2261 Bryant Street, San Francisco, CA 94110. 1-(415)-282-8900. Residential program with emphasis on low-income women in San Francisco. Six-month minimum stay for non-working women.

Alcohol and Drug Treatment Center at Stanford Medical Center, Department of Psychiatry, Room TF104, Stanford, CA 94305. 1-(415)-723-

6682. Fourteen beds, with a typical stay of thirteen days. Offers extensive outpatient care.

Foley House, 10511 Mills Avenue, Whittier, CA 90604. 1-(213)-944-7953. Residential program for twenty women and can take ten children. A thirty- to ninety-day program but can be up to six months.

Women's Alcoholism Program, 6 Camelia Avenue, Cambridge, MA 02139. 1-(617)-661-1316. Also treats drug addictions. Six-month inpatient care and outpatient programs, including group therapy.

Gosnold on Cape Cod, 200 TerHeun Drive, Falmouth, MA 02540. 1-(617)-540-6550. Two-week typical stay. Has seventy beds. Offers special women's program and outpatient care.

Gateway Rehabilitation Center, RD 2, Moffett Run Road, Aliquippa, PA 15001. 1-(800)-472-1177 (out of state, 1-[800]-472-4488). Offers a separate program for women. Typical stay twenty-eight days. Has more than ninety beds.

South Oaks Hospital, Alcoholism Program, 400 Sunrise Highway, Amityville, NY 11701. 1-(800)-732-9808. Inpatient and outpatient care in clinics. Also offers referral service.

Arms Acres Alcoholic Women's Program, P.O. Box X, Seminary Hill Road, Carmel, NY 10512. 1-(800)-227-2767 (out of state, 1-[800]-431-1268). In-hospital, residential treatment for alcohol and cross-addiction.

Mountainwood, 500 Old Lynchburg Road, P.O. Box 5546, Charlottesville, VA 22905. 1-(800)-468-3390 (out of state, 1-[800]-423-0541). Residential program. Can take up to seventy-four patients. Offers a cocaine treatment program designed for women.

The following organizations operate networks, with treatment programs across the country:

Parkside Medical Services, Park Ridge, IL. 1-(312)-698-4730.

Koala Centers, Nashville, TN. 1-(615)-665-1144.

Women for Sobriety, Quakertown, PA. 1-(215)-536-8026.

Alcoholics Anonymous, New York, NY. 1-(212)-686-1100.

The following groups offer hotlines and referrals:

National Institute on Drug Abuse, Rockville, MD. 1-(800)-662-HELP.

The National Cocaine Hotline: 1-(800)-COCAINE.

Woman to Woman (run by the Junior League), New York, NY. 1-(212)-355-4380 (in New York State, 1-[800]-ALCALLS).

National Council on Alcoholism, New York, NY. 1-(212)-206-6770.

Cocaine Anonymous, Culver City, CA. 1-(213)-839-1141.

Smoking

There are various methods used in many different types of programs available for those who want to quit smoking. It's best to do some research and decide what's best for your particular situation. The following organizations can refer you to local chapters or provide you with information on what's available in your area.

American Cancer Society, 4 West 35th Street, New York, NY 10001. 1-(212)-736-3030. Runs a two-week program within a support group.

American Lung Association, Box 598-MS, New York, NY 10001. 1-(212)-315-8700. Twenty-day self-help program.

American Medical Women's Association, 465 Grand Street, New York, NY. 1-(212)-477-3788. Provides information and referrals.

American Heart Association, 7320 Greenville Avenue, Dallas, TX 75231. 1-(214)-750-5300. Provides information.

Eating Disorders

The following organizations offer treatment. Check for cost and any specific requirements for admission:

American Health and Diet Company, 475 Park Avenue South, New York, NY 10016. 1-(212)-213-2430 (out of state, 1-[800]-828-7017). Conducts workshops and offers referral service.

Gracie Square Hospital Eating Disorders Program, 420 East 76th Street, New York, NY 10021. 1-(212)-222-2832 (out of state, 1-[800]-382-2832). Offers consultations, referrals, and an inpatient program.

South Oaks Hospital, Eating Disorders Unit, 400 Sunrise Highway, Amityville, NY 11701. 1-(800)-732-9808 or (516)-264-4000.

Bulimia, Anorexia Self-Help (BASH), 6125 Clayton Avenue, Suite 215, St. Louis, MO 63139. 1-(314)-567-4080 in Missouri; all other states 1-(800)-762-3334.

National Anorexic Aid Society, P.O. Box 29461, Columbus, Ohio 43229. 1-(614)-436-1112.

Overeaters Anonymous: Consult your local Yellow Pages.

The Renfrew Center, 475 Spring Lane, Philadelphia, PA 19128. 1-(215)-482-5353. A forty-bed facility on a 27-acre estate offers residential treatment for women. Forty-five- to sixty-day program.

Johns Hopkins Medical Institutions Eating Disorders Clinic, Meyer Building, 600 North Wolfe Street, Baltimore, MD 21205. 1-(301)-955-3863. Inpatient and outpatient treatment. Average stay is two and a half months, with aftercare.

UCLA Neuropsychiatric Institute Eating Disorders Program, 760 Westwood Plaza, Los Angeles, CA 90024. 1-(213)-825-5730. Offers inpatient and outpatient treatment.

University of Cincinnati Medical Center Eating Disorders Clinic, University of Cincinnati, Cincinnati, OH 45267-0559. 1-(513)-872-5118. Four-week residential program.

The following organizations provide information and referrals for treatment in your area:

National Association of Anorexia Nervosa and Associated Disorders (ANAD), Box 7, Highland Park, IL 60035. 1-(312)-831-3438.

National Anorexic Aid Society (NAAS), 5796 Karl Road, Columbus, OH 43229. 1-(614)-436-1112.

Overeaters Anonymous, P.O. Box 92870, Los Angeles, CA 90009. 1-(213)-320-7941.

American Anorexia and Bulimia Association. 133 Cedar Lane, Teaneck, NJ 07666. 1-(201)-836-1800.

Anorexia and Bulimia Resource Center, 2699 South Bayshore, Suite 800E, Coconut Grove, FL 33133. 1-(305)-854-0652.

Gambling

The following run workshops and can refer you to local treatment centers:

Gamblers Anonymous, National Service Office, P.O. Box 17173, Los Angeles, CA 90017. 1-(213)-386-8789.

National Council on Compulsive Gambling, 444 West 56th Street, Room 3207S, New York, NY 10019. 1-(212)-765-3833.

Gambling hotlines and referrals:

New Jersey Council on Compulsive Gambling 24-hour hotline: 1-(800)-GAMBLER.

Taylor Manor Hospital Hotline, Maryland: 1-(800)-LAST BET.

Compulsive Shopping/Spending

Debtors Anonymous General Service Board, P.O. Box 20322, New York, NY 10025-9992. Based on the AA program, using support groups. Can refer you to local chapters.

Shopaholics, Limited, 135 Willow Street, Apt. 207, Brooklyn, NY 11201. 1-(212)-484-0998 (leave a message if necessary). In Manhattan, offers workshops and support groups in a non-clinical atmosphere for New York area residents, and provides information nationwide.

Sexual Addictions

It is best to check with your local chapter of Alcoholics Anonymous for information on groups in your area that use the AA methods to help sexual addictions. There are some Sexaholics Anonymous chapters in major cities, but these are relatively new.

The American Association of Sex Educators, Counselors and Therapists will also help to guide you to a certified sex therapist or group therapy appropriate for your problem. Contact them at 11 Dupont Circle, NW., Suite 220, Washington, DC 20036-1207.

The Society for Sex Therapy and Research can also provide referrals:

S.S.T.A.R., Leonore Tiefer, Ph.D., c/o Beth Israel Hospital, Department of Urology, 10 Nathan D. Perlman Place, New York, NY 10003.

APPENDIX C

The Social Readjustment Rating Scale*

Life Event	Point Value
Death of spouse	100
Divorce	73
Marital separation	65
Jail term	63
Death of close family member	63
Personal injury or illness	53
Marriage	50
Fired at work	47
Marital reconciliation	45
Retirement	45
Change in health of family member	44
Pregnancy	40
Sex difficulties	39
Gain of new family member	39
Business readjustment	39
Change in financial state	38
Death of close friend	37
Change to different line of work	36
Change in number of arguments with spouse	35
Mortgage over $10,000	31
Foreclosure of mortgage or loan	30
Change in responsibilities at work	29

* Thomas H. Holmes and Richard H. Rahe, "The Social Readjustment Rating Scale," *Journal of Psychosomatic Research* 11 (1967), pp. 213–18.

Son or daughter leaving home	29
Trouble with in-laws	29
Outstanding personal achievement	28
Spouse begin or stop work	26
Begin or end school	26
Change in living conditions	25
Revision of personal habits	24
Trouble with boss	23
Change in work hours or conditions	20
Change in residence	20
Change in schools	20
Change in recreation	19
Change in church activities	19
Change in social activities	18
Mortgage or loan less than $10,000	17
Change in sleeping habits	16
Change in number of family get-togethers	15
Change in eating habits	15
Vacation	13
Christmas	12
Minor violations of the law	11

YOUR TOTAL:

In their sample poll in Seattle and from a Navy study of 2,500 subjects Holmes and Rahe found that people with scores over 300 points for one year had an 80 percent risk of becoming seriously ill or vulnerable to depression during the following year. Those with scores between 200 and 300 points still had an impressive 50 percent risk. Although these statistics cannot predict the risk for any particular individual, they do describe the correlation between life change and both physical and emotional health.

About the Author

GEORGIA WITKIN, Ph.D., is an assistant clinical professor at Mt. Sinai Medical College, Department of Psychiatry. She has had a private clinical practice for more than fifteen years and conducts special seminars for women on stress management and wellness around the country. She writes and lectures extensively and is on the board of *The Journal of Preventive Psychiatry* as well as the editorial advisory board of *Health* magazine. She lives in Manhattan.